Encyclopedia of COUNTRY Music

Left to right: *Elvis Presley and the Jordanaires,*
Roy Rogers and Dale Evans, Crystal Gayle,
Boxcar Willie

Encyclopedia of
COUNTRY
Music

Arthur Butterfield

GALLERY BOOKS
An Imprint of W. H. Smith Publishers Inc.
112 Madison Avenue
New York City 10016

This book was devised and produced by
Multimedia Publications (UK) Ltd

Editor: Jeff Groman
Production: Arnon Orbach
Design: John Strange and Associates
Illustrations by: Kevin Doherty
Picture Research: Sean Hogan, Don Roy

ISBN 0 8317 2793 4

First published in the United States of
America 1985 by Gallery Books, an imprint of
W. H. Smith Publishers Inc., 112 Madison
Avenue, New York, NY 10016

Typeset by Flowery Typesetters Ltd.
Origination by The Clifton Studio Ltd.,
London
Printed in Italy by Sagdos

Contents

Vernon Dalhart was one of the first singers to make a country record, in 1924.

Country music has reached us from many sources. The early settlers, mostly fleeing from Britain, brought with them the songs they had sung in their homelands – songs of love, war, adventure, work, and worship. Such songs seem to have flourished originally in the South, with the Appalachians forming the heartland. In time, the isolated, impoverished, God-fearing dirt farmers of Appalachia came to be known as 'mountain people' – a term that was later debased to 'hillbillies'.

Down in the southwest, Spanish influence spilled over the border, introducing Mexican hat dances and similar exotic rhythms. And French colonists in the bayous of Louisiana scraped their fiddles and push-pulled their accordions in a mishmash of French peasant dances, primitive jazz, and blues that later came to be called Cajun. While from the cottonfields of the South came the wail of African slaves – their days and nights of toil relieved by field shouts and hollers, their yearning for freedom voiced in spirituals and gospel music.

There were also cowboy songs. These grew from a fusion of Yankee adventure ballads and the lyric songs of the southern mountain people. Where these twin traditions met on the western plains, they spawned such classics as *Jesse James*, *Sweet Betsy from Pike*, and *Rye Whiskey*.

Came a time when folk singers began to make up their own words to borrowed tunes and thus emerged the first homespun American songs. Although much of the folk music of the early 1800s was a family affair restricted to the isolated communities and farmsteads of the South, song transmission, both oral and written, eventually spread throughout most of the settled regions of the continent.

At first the chief instrument used for song and dance accompaniment, as well as for solo work, was the exuberant fiddle. Cheap to make and buy, and invitingly portable, so popular did it become that fiddle contests and conventions held at various centers packed the whooping audiences in – as they still do to this day.

Slaves and their descendants later introduced a strange, three-string, plucked instrument that evolved into the essential five-string banjo. Some time afterwards the guitar, the third element of the oldtime string band, was introduced via the skilled fingers of black musicians.

Around the beginning of the 1900s, all-night barn dances, hoedowns, and square dances were accompanied by the everpresent fiddles. Banjos and guitars came as a bonus. Food and drink were spread out in never-ending quantities, and sugar was scattered on the floor before the session began. In the era before and during World War I,

Left: *Fiddlin' John Carson, oldtime fiddler and moonshiner from Atlanta, was first recorded by Ralph Peer in 1923. This disc became the first commercial record made for a specific market. It was aimed at fans of 'hillbilly' music and had unprecedented success.*

Below: *DeFord Bailey was a black harmonica player, with limited repertoire, who had the honor of opening the WSM Barn Dance program on 28th September 1928 – the night when George Hay gave it its new name of The Grand Ole Opry. Bailey played his version of* Pan American Blues.

individuals who were later to be immortalized in wax and on the air, were cutting their musical teeth at just such performances.

The titles of some of those dance tunes were as lively as the tireless steps themselves. Rosin flew to standards such as *Turkey in the Straw*, *Devil's Dream*, *Soldier's Joy*, and *Natchez under the Hill*. Some of these were later gratefully adopted by ace banjo and guitar pickers who transformed them into dazzling showpieces for their respective instruments.

Oldtime heroes

Who was the first country musician to be recorded? Discounting the occasional novelty fiddle numbers that found their way on to cylinders from 1909 onwards, there is still more than one claimant for the honor. Vernon Dalhart was arguably the first country singer to make a record, but when he was first recorded (from 1916 onwards) he was not a *country* singer. Dalhart (real name Marion Try Slaughter) was a light opera and ballad singer from Texas, and the songs he recorded were popular 'darkie' or 'coon' songs of the day. It was not until 24th August 1924, when he recorded *The Wreck of the Old 97* for Victor, together with *The Prisoner's Song* (his own adaptation of a traditional tune), that he decided that his future, after all, lay with country music.

Dalhart later partnered Carson J Robison, the Grand-daddy of Hillbilly Music and composer of such hits as the deadpan *Life Gets Teejus* and the rather more explicit *Barnacle Bill the Sailor*. Many winners were born from this collaboration, including *Way Out West in Kansas* and *My Blue Ridge Mountain Home*. Dalhart went on to record 5,000 releases under 100 pseudonyms.

The first truly rural, dyed-in-the-wool country musicians to be heard on record were probably Alexander 'Eck' Campbell Robertson and his pal, Henry Gilliland. Again from the Lone Star state, these were a couple of old-time fiddlers who, at the end of June 1922 (fully two years before Dalhart cut his disc), traveled from Richmond, Virginia, to New York City, Gilliland dressed up as a cowboy, and Robertson in Confederate Army uniform. They marched into the Victor premises and demanded a recording session. Possibly as the quickest way of getting rid of them as much as anything else, the Victor technicians acceded. In all, they cut six lively fiddle tunes, including *Sally Goodin* and *The Arkansas Traveler*. But these were not released until after the astonishing rival success of what must have been the first country *songs* (and, incidentally, the first country hits) to be recorded.

A break for Fiddlin' John
In the early 1920s, Ralph Sylvester Peer, talent scout and director of newly formed Okeh Records, had helped to establish a series of recordings that appealed to specialized markets – the so-called 'race' records, aimed mainly at black audiences. Such music consisted mostly of jazz and blues. Peer developed this idea still further by tapping regional centers for popular local talent, recording on location. In 1923, on one of his recording trips, he found himself in Atlanta, Georgia. At one session, the scheduled performer, a church singer, had unexpectedly dropped out. The local record distributor, Polk C Brockman, filled the gap by producing a popular character

Right: *Clayton 'Pappy' McMichen, pioneer fiddler, comedian, singer, songwriter, and bandleader, was one of Gid Tanner's Skillet Lickers in the 1920s when they made their definitive recordings of* Wreck of the Old 97, Sally Goodin, *and* Down Yonder.

Facing page: *Wade Mainer reads his requests on the air. Wade was an innovative banjoist who formed part of his elder brother J E's Mountaineers. He left in 1936 to lead his own group, the Sons of the Mountaineers. His most successful record was* Sparkling Blue Eyes.

Below: *Rare photograph of Gid Tanner and his Skillet Lickers, an outstanding string band of the 1920s and early 1930s. Apart from champion fiddler Tanner, they also included other fine musicians such as fiddler and songwriter McMichen, and blind guitarist Riley Puckett.*

called Fiddlin' John Carson, a champion fiddler and moonshiner from Georgia. Carson blithely fiddled and sang his way simultaneously through *Little Old Cabin in the Lane* and followed that with *The Old Hen Cackled and the Rooster's Goin' to Crow*. Peer was allegedly appalled at the resulting sound and would have preferred to forget the whole thing. But, because of an advance order from Brockman for the records, he pressed 500 without label or catalog number. When these were all snapped up by a wildly enthusiastic audience at an Atlanta old-time fiddlers' convention, Brockman promptly ordered and re-ordered thousands of extra copies. The manufacturers then decided to catalog them.

Thus, the first commercial records aimed specifically at a hillbilly audience were launched and took off in spectacular fashion. The recording date was 14th June 1923, and a new era for the industry had just dawned.

Carson's success inspired a rash of imitators who felt (sometimes with justification) that they could do better. Henry Whitter, a millhand from Virginia who embellished his vocalizing with harmonica and guitar, had actually recorded *The Wreck of the Old 97* and *Lonesome Road Blues* early in 1923, before Carson made his impact, but the recording company apparently did not consider them worth releasing. However, when Carson hit the jackpot, they had a change of heart. They persuaded Whitter to record nine more numbers, including the two they had previously shelved, and released them all in January 1924.

Ernest V 'Pop' Stoneman, a carpenter from Virginia, listened to Whitter's efforts and was convinced he could do better. He and his offspring eventually became one of

9

the most famous families in country music. A multi-instrumentalist on guitar, jew's harp, harmonica, banjo, and autoharp (he may have been the first autoharp plucker to be recorded), Pop was originally recorded by Ralph Peer in 1924. Those first few titles were released in 1925.

Pop Stoneman was prolific not only in his music-making but also in his conjugal duties. His heroic wife bore him 13 musical children, and in her spare time she played a mean fiddle with the band. Some 40 years on, the sound of the Stonemans (gospel songs, comedy numbers, old ballads, and bluegrass) was heard stronger and more joyfully than ever. In 1966 they were given their own TV show, and a year later won the Country Music Association Award for the Best Vocal Group.

Country pioneers
By 1925, a whole army of pioneer string bands and individual performers had begun to engrave their names on the record labels, and many of the major companies had set up special hillbilly series in their catalogues to meet the insatiable demands of their fans in the South. At that time such primitive country music was dubbed either 'hillbilly' (a faintly contemptuous reference that is highly resented today), or 'hill country music', which was the more refined term favored by Ralph Peer. But allegedly he himself was the first to give this music its pejorative description in 1925. It is said that Al Hopkins, a defector from Whitter's Virginia Breakdowners, led a four-piece band with no name. When asked at their recording session what they called themselves, Hopkins retorted that they were just a bunch of hillbillies from North Carolina and Virginia. Peer immediately christened them The Hill-Billies.

The Skillet Lickers were a rough, exuberant group made up basically of Gid Tanner, Riley Puckett, and Clayton McMichen. Two notable extras were Fate Norris, a fine banjo player, and Ted Hawkins, who dou-

Left: *Riley Puckett, blind guitarist, was first heard on radio in 1922, with Clayton McMichen's Hometown Boys. Two years later, he joined Gid Tanner and the Skillet Lickers. Besides playing guitar, Riley was featured vocalist with the group. In some of his later solo discs, he pre-empted Jimmie Rodgers with his yodeling.*

Facing page: *J E Mainer, elder brother of Wade, was the founder and leader of J E Mainer and his Mountaineers. Early on, he graduated from banjo to fiddle, on which he became an expert. In the 1930s he and his band were frequent and popular broadcasters, having changed their name to J E Mainer's Crazy Mountaineers.*

Below: *The Stoneman Family, led by Ernest V 'Pop' (with autoharp), were a much loved, early semi-bluegrass group who played and sang ballads, gospel, and other traditional material on a wide variety of instruments. Pop fathered 13 children, most of whom were musicians, and who were still performing in the 1980s.*

THE STONEMAN FAMILY

DELMORE BROTHERS
SONG FOLIO

CONTENTS

★

★ BLUES STAY AWAY FROM ME

★ MOBILE BOOGIE

★ SHE LEFT ME STANDING ON THE MOUNTAIN

★ PAN AMERICAN BOOGIE

And 14 Other Favorites

EXCLUSIVELY ON KING RECORDS

PRICE 60¢

Lois MUSIC PUBLISHING CO.
1540 BREWSTER AVE
CINCINNATI 7 OHIO

bled on mandolin and fiddle. Tanner was a burly Georgian chicken farmer who played fiddle. He had long been popular at fiddlers' conventions and was as much admired for his corny humor as his playing. He was more often than not to be seen and heard with his blind partner, guitarist and singer Riley Puckett.

Clayton McMichen was a car mechanic whose jazz-oriented fiddle style prefigured the wizardry of Stefane Grapelly. Tanner, Puckett, and McMichen, ably supported by Fate Norris – these formed the unlikely nucleus of the most successful early string band ever to be recorded. *Turkey in the Straw, Watermelon on the Vine*, and *Bully of the Town* were among the hits that sent their disc sales soaring into the hundreds of thousands.

A popular and important band of the 1920s and 1930s owed its genesis to J E Mainer, a cottonmill hand from North Carolina. A fine fiddler, he formed a semi-pro band about 1922. With him were his younger brother Wade on banjo, Zeke Morris on mandolin and guitar, and Papa John Love also on guitar. In 1932 they turned fully professional and began regular radio work. They called themselves J E Mainer's Crazy Mountaineers, after their first sponsor, the Crazy Water Crystals Company. With their instrumentals, ballads, and gospel music they formed a link between the string band sound of the 1920s and the vocal star era of the 1930s.

J E's brother Wade, besides contributing a distinctive vocal line, was also an expert two-fingered banjoist. This exciting overall sound helped to sell huge quantities of records and prefigured the early bluegrass style of the Monroe brothers. Wade parted from his elder brother around 1936 and formed an outfit which he called Wade Mainer and the Sons of the Mountaineers. Their greatest hit was *Sparkling Blue Eyes*, recorded in 1939 on the Bluebird label.

Another influential pioneer was the brilliant but alcoholic Charlie Poole from North Carolina. This banjo-

Left: Many of the original hillbilly musicians were raised on farms, part of a large family living in a log hut and helping to scratch a living from a few dirt acres. In their spare hours they perhaps practiced on a harmonica, a cheap Sears guitar, or a home-made fiddle, in order later to entertain friends and neighbors.

Facing page: Alton and Rabon Delmore, singers, fiddlers, and guitarists, were a highly popular radio, recording, and Opry duo in the 1930s and 1940s. Rabon, the elder, is credited with writing more than 1,000 songs, although they co-wrote their greatest hit, Blues Stay Away from Me, *which was in the charts for 23 weeks.*

Below: The influence of black musicians on some of the early white radio and recording stars was considerable. Jimmie Rodgers had unmistakable black country blues imagery in many of his verses, and he often included black sidemen in his later recordings, while Hank Williams owed much to a black street singer called Tee-tot.

Right: *Ralph Sylvester Peer in the 1920s was authorized by Okeh Records to scout for talent in the South. His first real success came in 1923, when he recorded Fiddlin' John Carson. Four years later, working for Victor, he hit the jackpot when he recorded both Jimmie Rodgers and the Carter Family for the first time within a few days of each other.*

Below: *In the 1800s, with the West still largely untamed, the cowboy became invested with a romantic charisma that has never quite been dispelled. The hundreds of ballads imputed to him by Hollywood and Tin Pan Alley scribblers, as he rode the trail, bore little relation to fact. Songs there were, but these were for the most part rough and repetitious.*

playing, singing, ex-mill hand began his brief musical career after teaming up with Posey Rorer, a crippled coalminer who played the swingingest fiddle in West Virginia. Guitarist Norman Woodlieff joined them later to form the North Carolina Ramblers. They waxed their first discs in 1925, for Columbia, and these were chiefly remarkable for one song – *Don't Let Your Deal Go Down*, which much later featured in the repertoire of Joan Baez and many others.

They played for the love of dear life
A few other groups and individuals from that freewheeling era deserve a mention. Dick Burnett and Leonard Rutherford formed an old-time fiddle and banjo duo who produced some memorable sides during their brief re-

cording careers. Burnett, a singer/songwriter and multi-instrumentalist from Kentucky, had the misfortune to be shot and blinded by a robber in 1907, at the age of 24. He joined fiddler and fellow Kentuckian Leonard Rutherford in 1914. Rutherford was also a good singer, and with Burnett's strong instrumental backing, they recorded their first discs, for Columbia, in 1926. Three firm favorites from their repertoire were *Short Life of Trouble, She's a Flower from the Fields of Alabama*, and the rhythmic *Billy in the Low Ground*.

Bradley Kincaid, The Kentucky Mountain Boy, pioneered Kentucky mountain music on radio in the early 1920s. Originally a banjoist, guitarist, and folk singer, he was mainly re-

sponsible for introducing Southern country music into the Northeast. Kincaid's first recording session, for Gennett, took place in 1928, and thereafter his name appeared on virtually every important label. His numerous links with radio were rivaled only by his appearances at every major barn dance.

The Carolina Tar Heels were an influential group of old-time musicians, made up at various times of guitarist and banjoist Clarence 'Tom' Ashley (of whom more anon), bluesy harmonica player Gwen Foster, Garley Foster 'the human bird' (no relation), and banjo wizard Dock Walsh. Ashley, Walsh, and Garley Foster had fine voices and were soloists in their own right. Foster's harmonica could bend

Facing page, top: *Bradley Kincaid, The Kentucky Mountain Boy, was an early star of the Grand Ole Opry. He began his radio work in 1925, singing the folk songs and authentic Kentucky mountain songs on which he had been raised.*

Right: *Jimmie Rodgers, the Singing Brakeman, occupies a unique place in the history of country music. With new means of communication his art reached and touched the lives of millions of Americans. It brought a bond of unity that helped sustain them through the grim years of the great Depression.*

Below: *J E Mainer's Mountaineers boasted within their ranks some outstanding performers. Among them* (top left) *was Clyde Moody, whose* Shenandoah Waltz *later sold some three million copies. The Mountaineers were one of the favorite string bands of the 1930s and early 1940s, and went on to cut more than 200 sides for RCA.*

notes in full flight and amply replaced the traditional fiddle sound. And the picking of Dock Walsh ('Banjo King of the Carolinas') on the 5-string is said to have inspired Earl Scruggs to develop his own world famous three-finger style. Their first joint recording session took place in 1927, for Victor. There were further sessions in 1931 (for which they called themselves the Pine Mountain Boys) and in 1932.

Clarence 'Tom' Ashley, a founder member of the Tar Heels, was a mountain banjoist and guitarist from Tennessee. His real name was Clarence Earl McCurry, and he began his musical career by busking for dimes in the streets, sometimes accompanied by Henry Whitter's blind recording partner, George Grayson. Later, as one of the entertainers with a traveling medicine troupe, Ashley helped to teach Roy Acuff some of the tricks of the trade when he eventually joined the same show. During the 1960s, along with a few other old-timers, he was rediscovered by musicologists and recorded two very fine albums: *Music at Clarence Ashley's, Volumes I and II.*

A stricken star: Jimmie Rodgers
Close to the end of the hillbilly era, two names – one of an individual, the other of a group – came to the country music surface and quickly towered

above the rest of the field. One was Jimmie Rodgers, the other was the Carter Family. And it is fitting that Ralph Peer, that country music disc-hound with the scent of success in his nostrils, should have recorded their respective debuts within four days of each other.

To many, James Charles Rodgers, variously called the Father of Country Music and the Singing Brakeman, was and *is* country music personified. He was born at Meridian, Mississippi, 8th September 1897. At the age of 14, with little formal schooling, Jimmie took a humble water-carrier's job on the railroad. His chores lay mainly among black workers who taught him to strum on banjo and guitar. He also learned something of their musical phrasing, the break in their voices, and how they sang the blues.

For 14 years Jimmie led a nomadic life, mostly in the Southwest, and was at different times assistant section foreman, flagman, and brakeman on the railroad. During that time he learned to yodel and to live with all sorts and conditions of men. He married in 1920, fathering a daughter a year later. When his second child died tragically, aged six months, he was in New Orleans and had to pawn his banjo to attend the funeral.

By that time, the specter of tuberculosis had begun to overshadow his every activity, and in 1925 he was finally forced to quit the railroad in search of less demanding labor. Hoping for relief in a better climate, he moved from Meridian to Asheville, North Carolina, but life was still pinched and precarious. Apart from a brief period as a store detective, Jimmie's days were spent mainly as an entertainer, singing and playing wherever he could find anybody to listen. He blacked up for a wandering minstrel show and later formed his own small string band.

In August 1927 Ralph Peer was in Bristol, Tennessee, touting for fresh phonograph talent. Jimmie turned up at the hotel for a solo audition (his band having earlier secretly defected for their own audition). He sang *The Soldier's Sweetheart,* an outdated sentimental World War I ballad, which he had reconstituted to call his own, and a yodeling lullaby, *Sleep, Baby, Sleep.* He would have liked to record one more side, with his original yodel, *T for Texas,* but Peer would have none of it. Nevertheless, Peer was sufficiently impressed with what he'd heard to hand Jimmie a contract, and promised to get in touch with him again soon.

Jimmie moved off to Washington, DC, and awaited that all-important call from Peers. At last, hearing nothing, he traveled to New York and demanded another recording session. This time he was allowed to sing four numbers, including *T for Texas.* It was originally titled *Blue Yodel,* the first of 13 numbered blue yodels. The song was a runaway hit and quickly sold a million copies. Within weeks Jimmie's royalty checks had swollen to more than $2,000 monthly. From then on he poured out a string of hits, including such favorites as *In the Jailhouse Now* and *Brakeman Blues.*

By that time Jimmie's popularity knew no bounds. His unsophisticated lyrics, quavering yodel, and mix of blues, earthy folk songs, and 'whitened' black music had a national appeal. And it was not long before his fame spread to other parts of the world. Foreign fans allegedly flocked to learn English in order to find out

Right: *Film extras wait their turn to face the camera during the shooting of a Hollywood B movie. Such films proliferated in the 1930s, but the action, however animated, never failed to freeze while the chosen singing cowboy (Autry or Roy Rogers, perhaps) warbled his mandatory ditty under Western skies.*

Bottom right: *Although Jimmie Rodgers was usually featured with a guitar in his hands, the backroom boys dreamed up all kinds of accompaniments for his singing. They included jazzmen, harmonica blowers, and Hawaiian bands.*

Left and below: *Bluegrass festivals, fiddlers' conventions and folk festivals in days gone by as now, never failed to attract capacity crowds.*

The Singing Brakeman.

Above: *Clapboard stores selling a variety of basics were a feature of the Old West.*

Facing page, far right: *The fiddle was the first and firm favorite of oldtime musicians because it was cheap to buy, easy to make, and convenient to tote around. But some of today's instruments can cost several thousand dollars.*

Facing page: *'Mother' Maybelle Carter, in addition to developing her own much copied guitar style, was also known as Queen of the Autoharp. She survived into the 1970s to play her autoharp on a classic triple album with Roy Acuff and others, called* Will the Circle Be Unbroken.

what Jimmie Rodgers was singing about. When Peer found out that Jimmie was also a songsmith (many of his numbers were written in collaboration with his prolific sister, Elsie McWilliams), instead of relying on traditional material as had country and folk artists before him, the wily talent scout grew even more excited. Peer promptly became his manager and began to look around for a more sophisticated backing than Jimmie's homespun guitar or banjo. As a result, an astonishing procession of groups and instruments were tried out and recorded behind Jimmie's voice, ranging from jazz groups to a musical saw.

Peer also shrewdly changed the image of his new protégé. Gone was the old hillbilly look, and in its place Jimmie wore a dapper railroad uniform or an immaculate white suit complete with pricey stetson.

Jimmie's driving determination to be famous and get rich quick seemed to be paying off. He was soon in traffic-jamming demand at theaters, concerts, and tent shows throughout the South and Southwest. He appeared on radio and even made a

10-minute movie, *The Singing Brakeman*. Strangely, he never trod the boards of the Grand Ole Opry. Within two years of his first recording as a down-and-out drifter, he had built himself a sumptuous $50,000 mansion at Kerrville, in Texas, his adopted state.

The only thing that defied him in his years of triumph was his insidious illness. His preoccupation with the problem was recorded in *TB Blues* and *Whippin' That Old TB*. He eventually grew so frail and wasted that engagements had frequently to be canceled; and the heavy cost of his lavish life style, and mounting medical bills, eventually forced him to quit his dream house.

In the early summer of 1933 Jimmie was visibly dying, but he insisted on returning to New York for a final recording session. A special cot was rigged up so that he could rest between takes. Over a period of eight days he managed to cut 12 sides. His last song, *Fifteen Years Ago Today*, was recorded on 24th May. Two days later he was dead.

Jimmie Rodgers was the first of

country music's commercial superstars. Although he made a lot of money and sold a lot of records, his sales were but a modest reflection of the lasting influence his songs and style were to have on many of his successors. Unabashed imitators (early in their respective careers) included such country music giants as Gene Autry, Ernest Tubb, and Hank Snow.

Jimmie Rodgers was one of the first three individuals to be elected to the Country Music Hall of Fame, and every year in his memory a Jimmie Rodgers celebration in Meridian draws huge crowds from every state in the nation.

The most musical family

Unlike Jimmie Rodgers, the Carter Family sought neither publicity nor wealth, but their influence on country music was just as far-reaching and durable, if not more so. Farmer and fruit salesman A P (Alvin Pleasant) Delaney Carter, a frustrated fiddle player who sang a somewhat tenuous bass in the local choir at Maces Springs, Virginia, was an ardent collector of Appalachian folk songs. These he would rework and some-

Right: *The legendary Carter Family was made up of Alvin Pleasant (A P); Sara, standing with autoharp; and 'Mother' Maybelle, seated with guitar. Known as Country's First Family, they popularized such standards as* Wildwood Flower *and* The Wabash Cannonball. *A P claimed many of these songs as his own, but what he did was to collect traditional material from the mountain folk and rework it for the trio.*

Facing page: *Carson J Robison was an extraordinarily popular songwriter and performer who was active from the early 1920s until his death in 1957. He was the composer of songs such as* Open Up Them Pearly Gates, *and comic offerings such as* Barnacle Bill the Sailor *and* Life Gets Teejus. *In the 1920s he teamed up with the legendary Vernon Dalhart, singing duets and providing guitar accompaniment.*

Above: *The life of the cowboy was not totally concerned with fighting off rustlers and serenading the several ladies of his choice by moonlight. Usually it meant long hours in the saddle during dusty days of herding cattle over hundreds of miles of rugged country, and coping with stampedes, drought, and disease.*

Right: *Later generations of the Carter family, with daughters joining their mother in a typical ensemble, made brave attempts to carry on the old tradition. But in a brash new world of electrified and amplified instruments, pop incursion, and rampant commercialism, the attempt was somewhat anachronistic and doomed to gentle failure.*

times claim as his own.

In 1915 AP fell in love with Sara Dougherty, a sloe-eyed beauty who lived on the other side of Clinch Mountain, and married her. Sara played guitar, tickled an autoharp, and charmed her hearers with her dark brown voice. She and AP played and sang duets, mostly old-time ballads and gospel numbers, at local mountain gatherings.

Some 10 years later, AP's brother Ezra married Sara's cousin Maybelle Addington, and brought his bride back to live near the Carters at Maces Springs. Maybelle joined Sara and AP in their playing and vocalizing and thus was born that vocal close harmony trio known to the world as the Carter Family. Sara sang lead, AP chipped in with bass continuo (which occasionally but regrettably tended to sound like the bleatings of a distressed sheep), and Maybelle produced a sweet alto harmony. Maybelle later came to be known as Mother Maybelle, Queen of the Autoharp. Besides singing, she developed some nifty licks of her own on banjo, autoharp, and especially guitar.

In the summer of 1927 the Carters, like Jimmie Rodgers, heard of Ralph Peer's recording sessions in Bristol and decided to try their luck. On 1st August, Peer was faced with a hillbilly group comprising AP and Sara and their three children, and a highly pregnant Maybelle. They were poorly dressed, dusty and mud-caked after their 25-mile journey, and Peer reluctantly got down to business. They recorded six sides that day, with Sara on 8-bar autoharp and Maybelle on guitar. Among the songs they sang were *Single Girl, Married Girl, Storms Are on the Ocean,* and *Bury Me under the Weeping Willow.* As soon as Peer heard Sara's lead voice he knew he was on to a winner.

Their records sold spectacularly well and persuaded them that the phonograph might well be their salvation, but they had to wait until the spring of 1928 before they were asked to wax any more sides. This time, in

23

Camden, New Jersey, they completed a dozen sides that included a number of standards that would forever be associated with the Carter Family – such items as *Wildwood Flower, Anchored in Love,* and *Keep on the Sunny Side.* While A P solemnly appended his name to these compositions (and Peer lost no time in slapping a copyright on them for his Southern Publishing Company), most of them had merely been collected by A P and then reworked and adapted to suit the trio. *Anchored in Love Divine,* for example, was an old hymn, and *Wildwood Flower* (which, with variations became a guitar-picker's show-off piece) was originally an old song with its roots in England.

Unlike Jimmie Rodgers, the Carters received little or no help from Peers and the record companies as far as publicity went. They organized their own shows throughout the rural South, pinning their handbills to trees, barn doors, and telegraph posts.

Jimmie Rodgers and the Carter Family did not meet during that first historic recording session in Bristol. This privilege was reserved for a later session in Louisville, Kentucky, in 1931. There they recorded together such numbers as *Hot Time in the Old Town Tonight* and *My Clinch Mountain Home.*

In spite of the group's growing fame, A P was already feeling the pinch by 1929 and drifted to Detroit, looking for work, while Maybelle and Ezra moved to Washington. Sara divorced A P in 1935 and four years later married Coy Bayes, AP's cousin. But in spite of domestic problems, the Carter Family regularly met together for recording purposes.

In 1943 they disbanded, after 14 years of work. Maybelle and her three daughters formed an act that continued until Maybelle's death in 1978. The youngest daughter, June, married Johnny Cash and has established a secure niche for herself in country music. The Carter Family were elected to the Country Music Hall of Fame in 1970.

Facing page: *In 1930 Jimmie Rodgers did a screen test for a possible film with cowboy philosopher and humorist Will Rogers (right), who claimed to be a fan of the Singing Brakeman's. The movie never materialized, but a year later the two performed together in a series of concerts for the victims of the Dust Bowl disaster.*

Below: *Fiddlers' conventions, apart from being fun, have a serious side in showing off various styles of folk fiddling. Texas fiddlers, for example, use a slightly legato technique that allows them to play more notes per bow stroke than the Eastern fiddlers. They, in contrast, use shorter bow strokes. The Canadian style betrays its strong Celtic roots in that it was originally used to accompany clog dancing, and some oldtime Canadian fiddlers still tap out the clog rhythms with their feet as they sit.*

The Grand Ole Opry: Curtain Raisers

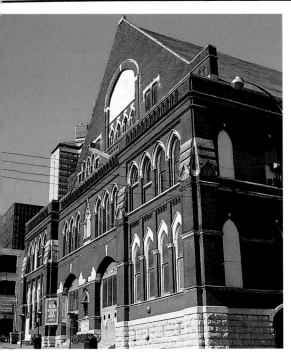

Above: *The Ryman Auditorium in Nashville was the home of the Grand Ole Opry for more than 30 years, beginning in 1941.*

Facing page, far right: *Opryland, the home of the Grand Ole Opry since 1974, is a music theme park located nine miles out of Nashville. The park covers 120 acres and includes musical shows of various kinds and rides such as carousels and roller coasters. The Opry itself is housed in the custom-built Opry Theater.*

The date was 10th December 1927: the occasion a broadcast of the WSM Barn Dance from Nashville, Tennessee. Announcer George Hay, hard on the heels of a classical music program, intoned: 'For the past hour we have been listening to Grand Opera – but from now on we will present the Grand Ole Opry.' That casual ad lib turned out to be an historic baptismal. It was a name that stuck, and it gave identity to a country music institution that has spanned 60 years of unbroken weekly radio broadcasts which, from humble origins, has blossomed into a multi-million dollar enterprise. Nearly 40 million listeners tune in weekly to the syndicated show, and the Grand Ole Opry House at Opryland, Tennessee, is usually packed to its 4,400-seat capacity each weekend.

George Dewey Hay (the 'Solemn Old Judge', as he styled himself at the ripe age of 30) was originally a reporter on the *Memphis Commercial Appeal,* and later its radio editor. In 1924 he moved to Chicago to become chief announcer on Radio WLS (World's Largest Store, Sears Roebuck), where he helped to found the WLS Barn Dance, later better known as the National Barn Dance. Just around that time, the National Life and Accident Insurance Company had built an imposing new radio station, WSM (We Shield Millions), in Nashville, to help sell their insur-

ance. Casting around for the best talent they could find, they invited Hay to head southwards once more and take over the job of radio director of their new enterprise.

Hay was a first-class all-round radio announcer (he had previously won the *Radio Digest's* award as the nation's most popular announcer), and not particularly interested in hillbilly music. Once established in Nashville, he was not too impressed with the palm court-type fare being served up daily on WSM for the local community. But he did notice that whenever a rural string band or similar outfit appeared briefly on the air it drew an immediate and gratifying response.

Acting on a hunch, Hay invited local fiddler Uncle Jimmy Thompson to sound forth with a few old-time fiddle tunes. Thompson was a Civil War veteran, fast approaching his eighties, who was only too willing to oblige. And on 28th November 1925, accompanied at the piano by his niece Eva Jones, the old boy scraped happily away for a full hour. At the end of the period, when asked if he hadn't done enough, he replied that he was only just beginning to warm up. For good measure, he added that he had just won an 8-day fiddle contest, had memorized more than 1,000 tunes, and could 'fiddle the bugs off a sweet tater vine.' It is not recorded if his last two boasts were ever put to the test.

Below: *A Grand Ole Opry souvenir program highlights some of the stars appearing there over the years. They range from early regulars such as Uncle Dave Macon to later arrivals such as Charley Pride.*

Dr Humphry Bate and the Possum Hunters were just about the most popular of the early string bands to grace the Grand Ole Opry. Bate, a practicing physician, fronted the band with his spirited harmonica playing.

Close to the earth

The response to this experiment was overwhelming and convinced Hay that a show patterned after his Chicago Barn Dance would boost the ratings. Within a few months, a scheduled barn dance was being broadcast each week. As more and more persons tuned in, so the show grew. It was alloted more than three hours air time each Saturday night, and WSM spectacularly increased the power of its transmitters.

There was no shortage of talent. Would-be artists formed a long line for auditions even though they knew they were giving their services free. Later, in order to discourage competition from rival barn dances, a fee of one dollar a minute was offered. Even today, stars appear on the Grand Ole Opry not for the paltry fee but for the honor and official recognition that such an appearance implies.

Hay quickly realized that this must be a homespun show for homespun folk. One of his favorite admonitions to the cast was 'Keep it close to the earth, boys'. He had no illusions about exploiting the hillbilly image to the full. Sober citizens of Nashville who had never milked a cow and had rounded up even fewer – chemists, garage mechanics, waiters, salesmen, insurance agents – would turn up neat and tidy in their city suits, but before Hay would allow any of them on stage, off came their coats and hats and ties in exchange for overalls, farm clothes, and outlandish mountain garb. He also invented what he considered suitable names for the bands, in keeping with their hillbilly outfits. As a result, the audience was entertained by the Dixie Clodhoppers, the Fruit Jar Drinkers, and the Gully Jumpers, among others. One such renamed band was Dr Humphrey Bate and the Possum Hunters.

Dr Bate was a graduate of the Vanderbilt Medical School. He was also, in his off-duty hours, a virtuoso harmonica player. In his band was his 13-year-old daughter Alcyone, who sang and also played ukelele and piano. The Possum Hunters were the first string band to appear on the Opry, and the good doctor earned from Hay the soubriquet 'Dean of the Opry'.

Man of many parts

The first great solo singing star thrown up by the Grand Ole Opry was an aging, rolypoly banjo player, vocalist, and raconteur named Uncle Dave Macon, affectionately known as the Dixie Dewdrop. He appeared on stage carrying three banjos and wearing plug hat, gold false teeth, wing collar, and gold watch and chain threaded across his ample double-breasted vest. He spent his youth far back in the 1800s, and yet he survived to star in a TV show as late as 1952.

David Harrison Macon was born in Tennessee in 1870. His father, a retired Confederate officer, ran a boarding house in Nashville which catered mostly for traveling entertainers. It was in such surroundings that Uncle Dave first learnt to pick the banjo in his bewildering series of complex styles, and later built up his apparently bottomless fund of anecdotes, folk songs, ballads, comic ditties, and mountain melodies. When it came time to earn a living, he acquired a small farm, and in 1900 he established a haulage business (the Macon Midway Mule and Wagon Transportation Company) which he ran successfully until World War I. He commemorated this business venture in a well-known song, *From Earth to Heaven*, and later, during his variety tours, he would sometimes appear on stage in a little cart drawn by two mules.

Showbiz still pulled him like a magnet and he spent many hours entertaining friends and neighbors for free with impromptu sketches and comical routines. In 1918 he was spotted by a talent scout from Loew's Theaters and promptly booked into a Birmingham, Alabama, theater. Success was immediate and his stage career never looked back. In 1923 he met up with a lean, skilled fiddler and guitarist called Sid Harkreader, and the two of them formed a partnership that toured the southern vaudeville theaters to great acclaim.

29

In 1924 the duo accepted an invitation to record with Vocalion in New York. During the first session they waxed 14 sides. They returned a year later to complete another 28 sides. The records issued at that time included some of Uncle Dave's most enduring and popular songs – *Keep My Skillet Good and Greasy, Hill Billie Blues,* and that exuberant impression of an old-time hunt, *Fox Chase.*

In 1925 guitarist Sam McGee (of whom more later) joined Uncle Dave on stage and in the recording studio, and for some years alternated with Harkreader as Uncle Dave's partner. In 1926, at the age of 56, Uncle Dave joined the WSM Barn Dance (not yet recognized as the Grand Old Opry), and continued to tread its boards for the next 26 years, on and off.

Uncle Dave's repertoire was not only seemingly infinite but also extraordinarily varied in moral tone. One day he could be in his element recording with the rumbustious Fruit Jar Drinkers, and next day he would be just as energetically pouring his heart out in some gospel number with the Dixie Sacred Singers. He could switch, apparently without turning a hair, from rough and rowdy songs such as *Bully of the Town* to moralistic sermons such as *You Can't Do Wrong and Get By.* He also could not resist penning commentaries on contemporary social and political situations, reflected in such songs as *Farm Relief* and *Governor Al Smith.*

Uncle Dave, at the age of 70, went to Hollywood in 1939 to star with Roy Acuff in the film *The Grand Ole Opry.* In it he sang a duet, *Take Me Back to My Old Carolina Home,* with Dorris, one of his seven musical sons, which turned out to be one of the highlights of the movie. In the late 1930s and 1940s he toured with some of the most famous names in country music – among them Roy Acuff, the Delmore

Facing page: *George Dewey Hay, the self-named Solemn Old Judge, founded the Grand Ole Opry in 1927. On that date, in his opening announcement, he renamed the WSM Barn Dance, calling it the Grand Ole Opry, and the name stuck. Hay continued to develop the Opry until the 1960s.*

Below: *Nashville, the home of country music, is not at first sight a particularly glamorous or attractive city. But its long association with legendary entertainers past and present, lends it an aura that is irresistible to country music fan and aspiring star alike.*

Brothers, and Bill Monroe. His last appearance for the Grand Ole Opry took place in March 1952, just three weeks before his death at the age of 82.

One of Uncle Dave's major contributions to the country music scene was his introduction of dozens of old-time ballads, folk songs, fiddle tunes, and banjo standards to later generations of entertainers. Such familiar numbers as *Arkansas Traveler, Soldier's Joy,* and *Cumberland Mountain Deer Chase* have firmly established themselves in the repertoire of many of today's star performers, and for this they owe Uncle Dave a debt of gratitude. His wide and continuing influence on country music was acknowledged in 1966 when he was elected to the Country Music Hall of Fame.

Sound of the blues

Brothers Kirk and Sam McGee were two more performers who helped to establish the Grand Ole Opry in its earliest days. Sam sang and played banjo and fiddle. His younger brother Kirk, consciously influenced by black musicians, became an expert guitarist. It was Kirk's old-time mountain guitar style, heavily spiced with the blues and ragtime, that brought a fresh flavor to the somewhat routine sound of the old-time string bands. It was especially effective in numbers such as *Railroad Blues* and *Buck Dancer's Choice.* Sam also claimed (rather shakily) that he was the first to play an electric guitar on the Opry.

In 1924 Uncle Dave Macon, liking what he heard, persuaded the brothers to join his outfit, and it was with him that they first appeared on the Opry.

Six years later, the McGees joined fiddler Arthur Smith to form the Dixieliners – a highly professional trio whose technical expertise was warmly appreciated by the cognoscenti. Some of their regular numbers, such as *Beautiful Brown Eyes* and *More Pretty Girls Than One* have been appropriated by a gamut of folk singers and bluegrass performers ever since.

When Smith left them just before World War II, the McGees appeared at irregular intervals on the Opry with various musicians, including Hank Williams, Ernest Tubb, and Roy Acuff. They were back on their own again from the 1950s onwards, and continued to appear at folk festivals as a duo until 1975, when Sam was killed by a farm tractor, at the age of 81.

Black country artists of note have always been thin on the ground, Charley Pride notwithstanding. And yet the very first musician to appear on the Grand Ole Opry (as distinct from the WSM Barn Dance) was a black harmonica virtuoso by the name of DeFord Bailey. It was on that historic December day in 1927 when George Hay casually changed the name and identity of the Barn Show with his announcement. When the distinguished conductor Dr Walter Damrosch brought his NBC Music Appreciation Hour to a close, it was DeFord Bailey who was called upon by Hay to demonstrate his wizardry on the harmonica with a spirited rendition of the train song, *Pan American Blues.*

Born in Carthage, Tennessee, Bailey was stricken with infantile paralysis at the age of three, and this left him deformed. He was the first musician to record in Nashville, making a number of records for Victor in 1928. Bailey stayed with the Opry until 1941. He had only a limited repertoire in which *Pan American Blues, John Henry, Lost John, Fox Chase,* and *Davidson Country Blues* figured prominently. It was alleged that his disinclination to add to his repertoire finally led to his dismissal from the Opry, although during his 15 years there he appeared more times on the show than any other artist. He was a great favorite with cast and audience alike, and was adopted as the mascot of the Opry.

But it was not all sunshine and smiles for DeFord Bailey. Fifty years ago it was tough at the top for a black in the Southern states, and Bailey often found that he was refused admission into restaurants and hotels while on tour, and was subjected to other forms of racial prejudice. After he was fired from the Opry in 1941, he operated a shoeshine stand in Nashville for

Facing page, top: *The Callahan Brothers, Walter T 'Joe' and Homer C 'Bill', pose for the camera with their respective families. A highly popular duo of the 1930s, they broadcast frequently over the years and cut nearly 100 record sides, including much western swing.*

Facing page, bottom: *Bill Carlisle and the Carlisles were a group formed in the late 1940s after Bill had separated from his brother Cliff. Members of the Louisiana Hayride and the Grand Ole Opry, they had some notable hits, including* No Help Wanted *and* Is Zat You Myrtle?

The Country Music Hall of Fame and Museum was established in 1961 in Nashville by the Country Music Association. Its aim is to honor personalities who have made valuable contributions to country music, and each year there is a secret ballot to determine the voters' choice. The museum houses descriptive plaques of each member, together with a collection of memorabilia, including photographs, costumes, musical instruments, and other souvenirs.

many years, a sadly embittered man.

Growin' fit to bust

Meanwhile, the Opry itself was having to move from one location to another as it regularly outgrew its premises. Its first home was the small WSM studio on the fifth floor of the National Life and Accident Insurance Company building in Nashville. In order to placate the many fans who came to WSM hoping to catch a glimpse of their favorite radio stars, a special studio was built next door. In this, up to 500 persons could sight-see for free through a plate-glass window. Soon, conditions became too crowded and the Opry moved to the rented Hillsboro Theater, a former movie house. But it was not long before it was bursting at the seams again, and the Opry found itself occupying a large rambling tabernacle in East Nashville, on the opposite side of the Cumberland River. For two years it performed there in great discomfort both for audience and cast. In spite of the less than welcoming splintery benches and sawdust-covered floor, the house was filled to capacity.

In 1939 there was another move, this time to the Tennessee War Memorial Auditorium, which held about 1200 persons. These lucky customers were charged 25 cents each admission fee in a vain attempt to reduce the overcrowding. In that year, too, the show was networked across the nation for the first time. Enormous audiences attended the live performances each week, so once again the removal men were forced to call. This time the Opry found refuge in the Ryman Auditorium, later renamed Opry House in the full expectation that this would be their permanent home. The imposing Victorian structure had been built in the early 1890s as a place of worship by a whiskey-toting, unbelieving riverboat captain, Tom Ryman, who had come to break up a holiness meeting and had stayed to pray.

Cold, damp, minus air conditioning, poorly repaired over the years, and eventually officially condemned as a fire risk, Opry House was finally abandoned in 1974. The show moved to a new 4,400-seat Opry House located in Opryland, a 369-acre entertainment park opened a couple of years earlier a few miles outside downtown Nashville. The park was designed to be 'The Home of American Music', has heavenly amenities, and cost the earth. The new Opry House is plush, luxurious, and convenient. New arrivals love it, but some of the old-timers shake their heads wistfully and sigh a little for the days when everything was 'good and country'.

Those who trod a quieter path

The formative years of the Opry – the late 1920s and 1930s – saw many pioneer country singers and pickers come and go, some of the most illustrious never even getting to tread the weather-beaten boards of the Opry itself, Jimmie Rodgers and the original Carter Family being prime examples.

An old-time traditional singer and banjo-picker who caused a mild sensation when he was rediscovered by Mike Seeger in the 1960s was Dock Boggs. Moran Lee 'Dock' Boggs was a Virginia coalminer who started cutting coal at age 12, and thereafter worked for nearly half a century underground before retiring. He said he only played banjo for fun. The truth was, his strictly religious wife was convinced that banjo-playing was a sure passport to hell fire and did all she could to discourage her husband's 'sinful music'. Dock started playing in his teens and developed a unique, three-finger, bluesy finger-picking style that followed the melody instead of forming an accompaniment. It evolved from several licks taught him by black musician friends. His haunting songs were a mixture of black and white material absorbed from wandering minstrels. In 1927, throwing conjugal caution to the winds, he recorded several sides for Brunswick. From then on, he found he was much in demand at various folk fests in the South.

Close harmony duetists began to come into their own in the early 1930s, usually relying on guitar and mandolin for accompaniment. The Callahan

Brothers, Homer and Walter, were just such a popular duo. They came from North Carolina originally, but headed steadily southwestwards as they toured, and finally ended in Dallas. Once there, they suddenly and unaccountably changed their names to Bill and Joe, respectively. By 1933 they were already established radio stars, and they later recorded a number of sides for ARC and Columbia. More and more they drifted into cowboy music and western swing. They made music together until the 1960s, but after Homer's (Bill's) death in 1971, his brother opted for professional photography in Dallas.

Kentucky comics

The Carlisle Brothers were country music duetists notable mainly for starting a new trend in that genre. Instead of hewing to the accepted pattern of close harmony singing, they preferred to belt out their numbers in wild abandon, spiced with expert yodeling and the whine of the dobro.

(The dobro is a guitar with raised strings and a metal resonator. It is played horizontally, and its sound is akin to that of the Hawaiian guitar. It was devised in 1925 by Ed and Randy Dopyera, and took its name from the DOpyera BROthers). The Carlisles came from Wakefield, Kentucky, sons of a musical family working on a tobacco farm. Cliff, the elder, left home at a tender age and joined a vaudeville circuit. There he collected much of his later bawdy repertoire, learnt to yodel, and became one of the finest dobro and steel guitar players of his time.

In 1930 Cliff joined guitarist Wilbur Ball, the two of them recording some memorable duets for Gennett, including blues, some blue material, and Hawaiian-type music. When Jimmie Rodgers heard them on radio, he was so impressed that he invited them to form part of his backing group for his next recordings. So it was that in 1931 Cliff played steel guitar and Wilbur acoustic guitar with Rodgers in recordings of *Looking for a New Mama* and *When the Cactus Is in Bloom*. Cliff later teamed up with guitarist and yodeler Fred Kirby and in so doing launched one of the first yodeling duos in country music. Younger brother Bill eventually joined Cliff and the pair continued with the previous pattern of bawdy songs, blues, gospel numbers and comedy routines. From about 1930 onwards, until Cliff retired in 1947, the Carlisle Brothers in one form or another were represented on just about every major record label in the country. They appeared with different partners and a variety of instrumentation in the Cincinnati and Lousiville areas, delighting their fans with numbers such as *Mouse's Ear Blues*, *The Girl in the Blue Velvet Band*, and *Rattlesnake Daddy*. They also starred in big radio shows, including Louisiana Hayride, Ozark Jubilee, and their own The Carlisle Family Barn Dance.

Facing page, top: *Patsy Cline was at one time a serious rival to Kitty Wells for the title of Queen of Country Music. She gained her first great success on the Arthur Godfrey Talent Scouts TV show in 1957 with* Walkin' After Midnight, *which later became her first recorded hit. Enormous hits followed in the early 1960s, including* Crazy *and* When I Get Thru with You, *but her life was tragically cut short in a plane crash on 5th March 1963.*

Facing page, bottom: *Grandpa Jones was a favorite performer both in Hee-Haw and the Opry. Although only a young man at the start of his career, he disguised himself as an old-timer, and with some brilliant banjo playing, offered a much-loved comedy routine.*

Below: *Ernest Tubb's record shop in Nashville was known the world over among country music fans. In 1947 he started a radio show, the Midnight Jamboree, from the store, which is now located in Demonbreun Street.*

After his brother retired, Bill formed his own family group, The Carlisles. They joined the Grand Ole Opry in 1953, and after that date Bill, alone or with his family, won nearly 70 awards. In 1953 *Too Old to Cut the Mustard*, and in 1954 *No Help Wanted* each won the accolade of Best Record of the Year. In 1955 Bill was voted Best Comedian of the Year, and in 1966 he scored again with the hit song *What Kinda Deal Is This?*

Two more Opry stars

The Delmore Brothers were altogether a different kettle of fish. Two young farm boys hailing from Elkmont, Alabama, they became pioneers of a close harmony style of playing and singing that kept them firm favorites in the Grand Ole Opry for nearly 10 years. Both excellent fiddlers, they chose to perform (unusually) with two lead guitars – a six-string and a tenor (4-string). They were among the first 'soft' singers to be heard in public, and their repertoire consisted of traditional songs (of which they knew a vast number), black-influenced, bluesy country music, and a type of country boogie. Their approach was highly professional, with soft, light harmonies and precise, accurate picking. In addition they were both prolific songwriters and performed much of their own material. Alton, the elder brother, penned more than 1,000 tunes, and Rabon more than 200.

Their first records were made for Columbia in 1931 and the following year they made their first broadcast for the Grand Ole Opry. Probably the most famous number was *Blues Stay Away from Me*, which they co-wrote, and which was recorded over and over again by later country stars. Other classics associated with them include *Brown's Ferry Blues, Beautiful Brown Eyes, Freight Train Boogie*, and *When It's Time for the Whipoorwill to Sing*.

After leaving the Opry, the Delmores were featured in many top country-style radio shows in Arkansas, Alabama, Indiana, and North and South Carolina. They made more records, some with Grandpa Jones, Merle Travis, and Red Foley. The part-

Facing page, bottom: *George Hay, emcee, welcomes Kitty Wells, Queen of Country Music, to the microphone at the Grand Ole Opry. Besides being a successful solo singer, Kitty also scored massive hits with singing partners such as Roy Acuff, Red Foley, and Webb Pierce.*

Below: *The Blue Sky Boys* (on the left) *perform with Red Hicks. The Bolick Brothers, to give them their real name, were a superb close harmony duo who specialized in oldtimey and religious songs during the 1930s and early 1940s. Postwar audiences preferred something different.*

nership was broken with the death of Rabon in 1952 with lung cancer. Alton, who had shown signs of incipient alcoholism, taught guitar until his death some 12 years later. In 1971 the Delmores were posthumously elected to the Songwriters' Hall of Fame.

Monroe Brothers: begetters of bluegrass

The Monroe Brothers were another duo who came into prominence in the 1930s. Their style of picking and singing laid the foundations for a volcanic phase of country music, called bluegrass, that was to erupt in the 1940s.

The Monroes were a family of eight children from Rosine, Kentucky. Charlie was the seventh child and Bill the eighth and youngest, although there was an eight-year gap between their ages. Bill was a lonely boy with poor eyesight and something of an introvert. Working alone out on the fields of the family farm, he was able to exercise his lungs and musical talents for long hours at a time with nobody to disturb him. Bill quickly

Right: *In the late 1930s and 1940s dance halls proliferated in many parts of the South, especially Texas. Bob Wills and his Texas Playboys and other Texas swing bands filled the ballrooms with perspiring couples determined to enjoy their Saturday night out. From these origins evolved the more strident honky tonk saloons. The names, if not the function of some of these early dance halls, have been retained or revived in modern times.*

Facing page: *Uncle Dave Macon began his professional career in the early 1920s and very soon came to be acknowledged as the complete entertainer, even though by that time he was already middle-aged. He laced his act with songs, banjo solos, and humorous anecdotes. and for many years was a must on the Grand Ole Opry. In addition to his eagerly awaited solo routine, he also formed part of a fun-loving band called the Fruit Jar Drinkers.*

learnt to play guitar and mandolin. Charlie also took up guitar and another brother, Birch, excelled on the fiddle. Another great fiddler was Bill's Uncle Pendleton Vandiver (Bill later paid tribute to him in his famous bluegrass composition, *Uncle Pen*). Bill and Uncle Pen would sometimes play for local square dances, providing guitar and fiddle accompaniment.

The three brothers, Birch, Charlie, and Bill found manual jobs by day in East Chicago, Indiana, and by night played at dances or amateur get-togethers. At around that time Bill abandoned the guitar for the mandolin and became the acknowledged master of the instrument in terms of country music. In 1934 Birch gave up music and left the trio. Bill and Charlie formed a mandolin/guitar duo, working with the WLS Barn Dance show.

Their first historic recording was made on the Bluebird label in 1936. One side featured an old gospel favorite, *What Would You Give In Exchange for Your Soul?*, and the other highlighted another religious offering, *This World Is Not My Home*. They went on to record 60 songs for Bluebird in the intervening two years before they went their separate ways in 1938.

The music of the Monroe Brothers was the fastest and most exciting and innovative ever heard by a country music audience up to that time. Charlie provided surging bass runs on guitar, but it was the astonishing, no-holds-barred, lightning fast licks all over the mandolin fingerboard that made the instrument a virtuoso solo performer in its own right for the first time. Such dazzling mastery, combined with Bill's high, driving falset-

to, had audiences and rival musicians awe-stricken. This new sound pioneered by the Monroes was to have a profound effect on bluegrass and other types of country music for years ahead.

After the break, Bill went on to form the first genuine bluegrass group (of which more later). Charlie, less flamboyant than his brother, nevertheless stayed with country music. He formed his own group, the Kentucky Pardners, which remained active until the 1950s. In the early 1970s he came out of retirement to play some welcome bluegrass for a while before his death in 1975.

Sunny side of life

The Blue Sky Boys (Bill and Earl Bolick) were another male duo who were broadcasting and recording around the mid-1930s, and who also

Below: *Opryland, USA, a musical theme entertainment park built just outside Nashville at a cost of several million dollars, houses not only the Grand Ole Opry but also plays host to many other musical shows, rallies, and exhibitions.*

41

made a deep impression on their audiences. The Bolicks (who felt that their name hadn't quite got the right ring to it and changed it to the Blue Sky Boys for professional purposes) hailed from Hickory, North Carolina. They were mere teenagers when they first started writing their own material and broadcasting over local radio stations. Bill, the elder, learnt banjo and guitar first, then taught guitar to Earl.

The Blue Sky Boys chose to sing religious songs, traditional folk songs, and Anglo-American ballads. Earl, with his deep voice, sang lead and played guitar; Bill sang tenor harmony and backed that with simple but effective mandolin. (He was forced to take up the mandolin by popular demand, because the Monroes were sweeping all before them with their mandolin/ guitar combination). They sang in a slow, deliberate, almost mournful way, their voices blending exquisitely, and admirably suited to their repertoire. Their style was in direct opposition to the Monroes' frontal attack, so there was no direct competition. Their theme tune and best known recording was *Sunny Side of Life*, an old gospel tune that was rearranged by Bill. It has since been recorded and played by just about every bluegrass and old-timey revivalist band worth its salt.

Their first recording session took place in the summer of 1936, with Victor. Among other favorite songs waxed in the 1930s were *Banks of the Ohio, The Butcher Boy, Who's Gonna Shoe Your Pretty Little Feet?* and *The Unquiet Grave*. They were at their peak when World War II broke out and robbed them of at least five very productive years. After the war, country music tastes had changed. The Blue Sky Boys refused to compromise with their style, even firmly rejecting the proposal that they should include an

Grandpa Jones (on the left) was much influenced by Uncle Dave Macon. Like him he switched from guitar to banjo and settled for a mixed comedy routine of oldtimey songs and Appalachian mountain anecdotes to an accompaniment of banjo and boisterous whoops and kicks. Besides his solo work, Jones also recorded with stars such as the Delmore Brothers and Merle Travis.

electric guitar in their act.

They parted company in 1951, still comparatively young men. One went to work for an airplane firm, the other joined the post office. They made personal appearance and recording come-backs in 1962 and 1963, again in 1965, and finally in 1975. Sadly, they achieved only mixed success with their records, in spite of a superb album for Capitol in 1965.

Smokey Mountain star

Roy Acuff, the King of Country Music, was the first truly successful singing star of the Grand Ole Opry, as distinct from string bands and singing duos. Roy Claxton Acuff was born in Maynardville, Tennessee, the son of a one-time Baptist minister, lawyer, postmaster, and farmer. His boyhood was spent in the beautiful Smokey Mountains, where he learnt to play jew's harp, harmonica, and fiddle.

The family moved to Knoxville and Roy, although physically wispy and slight, became a star athlete at High School there. So good a ball player was he that the New York Yankees considered signing him up. But a severe case of sunstroke incurred on a fishing trip ended his baseball dreams. A long two years of convalescence followed, during which Roy improved his fiddle technique, learnt to sing, mastered the yo-yo, and got thoroughly hooked on recorded versions of old-time country stars such as Charlie Poole and Gid Tanner.

In 1932 he joined Dr Hower's Medicine Show and toured with them throughout Tennessee and Virginia. This was a hard but invaluable school of experience in which Roy at one time or another played every part on the set, black and white, male and female. It was all fun to him, and he decided that the entertainment business was his for life. A year later he

The familiar rugged landscape in parts of Texas, Colorado and Wyoming, the sheer vastness of the territory, with its sweeping skies, awakened an emotive response in the hearts of greater and lesser poets. It gave rise to the 'lone prairie' type of song and invested the hard-riding cowboy with an aura of glamor and romance that has never died.

Facing page: The Blue Sky Boys, who first began recording in 1936, brought a professionalism to their work that was quite rare in the early string band days.

Below: The original hillbilly performers were glad to sing and play for nothing at the Grand Ole Opry. But gradually, live gigs and recording contracts produced artistes, whose names went up in lights.

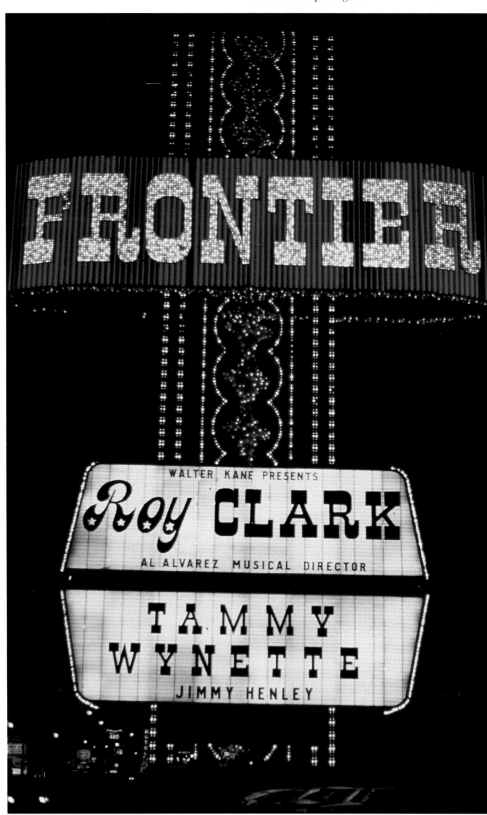

formed his own band, Roy Acuff and his Crazy Tennesseans, and began broadcasting from stations WNOX and WROL, and appearing at local concerts, socials, and hops. At that time Roy's program included some semi-pop, middle-of-the-road numbers of the day such as *Yes, Sir, That's My Baby*, mingled with more traditional ballads and some of his own songs. Not much later, he discarded all the pop material and stuck closely to what he knew and did best – singing traditional, religious, and moralistic songs with a mournful, wailing, mountain sound, in which he was helped by the dobro-playing of Bashful Brother Oswald (Pete Kirby).

His first recording session came with Columbia, in 1936. He changed the name of his outfit to The Smokey Mountain Boys and recorded two songs that have ever since been associated with his name and quickly brought him in his first million dollars: *Great Speckled Bird* and *The Wabash Cannonball*. He wrote the first song himself, to an old Carter Family tune, and later it became the name of his private airplane. The second number was his theme song, and so popular did it become that a train was eventually named for it. *The Wabash Cannonball* had grossed more than five million dollars at the latest count, and formed just a fraction of Roy's 25 million records sold by Columbia.

After five years of trying, Roy was at last accepted by the Grand Ole Opry in 1938, and from then on until after World War II he virtually *was* the Opry.

By that time his fame had spread abroad. In a poll of US service stations in Germany he displaced Frank Sinatra for popularity. A legend he takes pride in is that when the Japanese charged the US marines in Okinawa during World War II, they screamed what they hoped would be the most demoralizing insults: 'To hell with Roosevelt, to hell with Babe Ruth, to hell with Roy Acuff!'

In 1942 he helped to finance songwriter, publisher, and producer Fred Rose when he founded the Acuff-Rose

Music Publishing Company – an enterprise devoted exclusively to publishing country music. Hickory records also came under their wing in the 1950s. Among Roy's other commercial interests was Dunbar Cave, an entertainments center at Clarksville, Tennessee.

During the late 1940s Roy was persuaded to dabble in politics. He failed to get through the primaries when he ran for governor of Tennessee in 1944 and 1946. He won the Republican primary in 1948, although beaten in the election in a solidly Democratic region. It was during those years, too, that Roy produced some of his most memorable hits, including *Fireball Mail, Night Train to Memphis,* and *Wreck on the Highway.*

In 1952, under pressure form Columbia to change his style, Roy left the label to try his luck with Decca, MGM, Capitol, and his own Hickory marque. His live appearances attracted greater crowds than ever, and his music publishing flourished as never before, being largely responsible for making Nashville the music publishing hub of the world.

In 1965 he was badly injured in a road crash, but within a few months he was on the circuit once more. He even flew out to Vietnam to entertain the troops. In 1971 he joined with the unlikely combination of the Nitty Gritty Dirt Band, Mother Maybelle Carter, the fabulous blind guitarist Doc Watson, Earl Scruggs (Mr 5-string banjo himself) and a host of other stars in the United Artists 3-record set, *Will the Circle Be Unbroken.* Roy stole the show in this unique experiment, which deservedly won a gold disc award. In 1974, at the opening of the new Nashville Opryhouse, President Nixon was so taken with Roy's yo-yo technique that he asked for, and received, lessons.

Fred Rose, Roy's original partner in the music publishing business, died in 1954. He received a signal honor in 1961 when he was elected to the Country Music Hall of Fame, being one of the first three members (along with Jimmie Rodgers and Hank Williams). Roy Acuff achieved the unique distinction of joining that august company in 1962, the first living member ever to make it.

Facing page, top: *Roy Acuff demonstrates his famous balancing act with his fiddle bow on his chin. He also prides himself on his yo-yo technique.*

Facing page, bottom: *Roy Acuff's popularity on the Grand Ole Opry was rivaled only by that of Uncle Dave Macon. Leading his band, The Smoky Mountain Boys, with its distinctive dobro sound, the King of Country Music made a name*

for himself that was recognized from Alaska to Antarctica, and from Rio to Rangoon.

Below: *Roy Acuff was the first living musician to be honored by being elected to membership of the Country Music Hall of Fame. In 1942 he joined Fred Rose in organizing the prestigious Acuff-Rose music publishing company.*

3 Singing Cowboys

Facing page: *Gene Autry, the greatest of the singing cowboys, was made by the movies. Together with his horse Champion, he starred in dozens of B Westerns, and built up a massive total of recorded hits in the process.*

Perhaps no character in the Western world has had so much glamor, myth, and hokum heaped upon him by word, song, and film as the American cowboy. Old time heroes – soldiers, sailors, pirates, trackers, and Indian braves – had faded and been forgotten. Who could replace them in the 20th century imagination, fed on 'Western' dime novels, but the romantic cowboy? That lean figure, tall in the saddle, riding off into the sunset, was a natural. But of course, he had to sing.

The original, dyed-in-the-wool cowboys did sing, after a fashion. They hollered to their semi-wild longhorns by day to keep them on the hoof, and by night they soothed them with a kind of crooning. And the cattle seemed to enjoy it. This was odd because the oldtime cowpokes knew only about half a dozen tunes all told, and to these they fitted as many loosely scanning stanzas as would last the night out. Contrary to later impressions created by Autry, Rogers, and others, the guitar was conspicuous by its absence. It was inconvenient to tote and just about impossible to play in the saddle. Musical instruments ranged from few to none – at best, perhaps an old fiddle, harmonica, and jew's harp. Rhythms were tapped out in the dirt by the heel of the boot, and the cowboys' voices raised in song have been likened to 'a pack of coyotes howling'. *Sam Bass, The Old Chisholm Trail, The Buffalo Skinners, I Ride an Old Paint, Night Herding Song* (written in 1909 by a bored broncobuster in the wee small hours), and a few garbled hymns were typical of the limited stock-in-trade of the genuine cowboy who rode through the arid brush of southern Texas.

A number of recordings were made of such songs in the 1920s by so-called 'cowboy balladeers'. Among such performers was Carl T Sprague (The Original Singing Cowboy), from Houston, whose outstanding number, *When the Work's All Done This Fall*, recorded in 1925, sold nearly a million copies. Sprague was still recording as late as 1972. Jules Verne Allen (Longhorn Luke) was also one of this group of pseudo-cowboy balladeers. By trade he was a Texas cattle drover, and he is chiefly remembered for his recordings of *The Days of Forty-Nine* and *Zebra Dun*.

Harry 'Mac' McClintock (Haywire Mac), a Tennessean, as well as recording genuine cowboy songs such as *Sam Bass* and *Cowboy's Lament*, introduced an appreciative public to hobo ballads such as *Big Rock Candy Mountain* and *Halleluia, I'm a Bum*.

But it was Hollywood that paraded its own larger-than-life cowboys before millions of adoring fans. Tom Mix, William S Hart, Hoot Gibson and other stalwarts were necessarily silent in those early screen days. But in 1927, when Al Jolson was heard

Below: *Gene Autry originally billed himself as Oklahoma's Singing Cowboy. Included in his long list of massive recorded hits were* Silver Haired Daddy of Mine, Yellow Rose of Texas, *and inevitably,* Rudolph the Rednosed Reindeer.

talking and singing in *The Jazz Singer*, all that was abruptly changed. The first singing cowboy to be seen on screen was Ken Maynard, who in 1930 appeared in *The Wagon Master*. One of the songs he sang was *Cowboy's Lament*, but audience reaction was negative.

Almost unbelievably, the first moderately successful candidate among the singing screen cowboys was John Wayne. Needless to say, his voice failed to bring down the chandeliers but, regrettably from Wayne's point of view (who hated even trying to sing), the fans lapped it up, especially in rural areas. Wayne's first warbling role was that of Singin' Sandy, a singing US secret agent in *Riders of Destiny*. And from then on, every movie he made had to have at least two, three, or sometimes even four songs apiece, for Wayne's benefit. Wayne regarded it all as a rather tiresome gag, and was pretty sure that his tuneless voice would soon be relegated to strictly speaking parts. But when this didn't happen, he could stand it no longer. At the renewal of his contract he laconically informed the head of Republic Studios, 'Go get yourself another cowboy singer!'

The studio faced a dilemma. Auditioning singers who couldn't act or ride, and actors who couldn't ride or sing, they finally settled for a stocky, rather plain guy who sang not unpleasantly, had never acted before, and could ride although allegedly was not over-fond of horses. His name was Gene Autry.

Oklahoma adventure

Orvon Gene Autry was born in Tioga, Texas. With a baptist minister for a grandfather, young Gene soon learnt to sing hymns with the best of them. But by the time he was 17 he had added to his vocal repertoire by singing in local nightclubs for a few dimes at a time. He eventually joined Field Brothers' Medicine Show, playing saxophone and singing to his own guitar accompaniment. When his father bought a cattle ranch at Achilles, Oklahoma, Gene undertook to drive his cattle the short distance from

Below: *Gene Autry, the mòst popular of the singing cowboys of the 1930s and 1940s, invested his accrued millions with commendable acumen. Today he owns radio and TV stations, a record company, a hotel chain, a major league baseball club, and a music publishing company, among other assets.*

Opposite: Gene Autry (top) and Roy Rogers (bottom) each laid claim to the title King of the Cowboys. In truth, neither of them was a genuine cowboy but they aptly symbolized on celluloid a romanticized era that never was.

the farm to the railroad station. It was a far cry from the professional ball game, which had been his first ambition.

Trains fascinated him more than cows did and it was not long before he was learning morse code in order to take a telegraphist's job on the railroad. He was given a job (midnight to 8 a.m.) on the Frisco Line in Chelsea, Oklahoma, and one fateful night humorist and actor Will Rogers walked in to send a wire. Seeing Gene's guitar, he asked Gene to sing *They Plowed the Old Trail Under*. The telegraphist obliged and was rewarded with Rogers' version of *Casey Jones* in exchange. This was the first of several visits by Rogers, who encouraged the youngster to persevere with his singing and playing.

Gene took it all to heart and practiced for another three years then grabbing his guitar he made for New York. It was 1929, and all Gene had to offer was a generous selection of Jimmie Rodgers songs, a soft, nasal tenor voice, and a good blues yodel. In some songs his voice was quite indistinguishable from that of his idol. Gene waited for hours at the Victor offices and was finally auditioned and allowed to record for them briefly as Oklahoma's Singing Cowboy. He also cut a few sides for ARC. But the verdict was that he should try working on radio for a year or so first, in order to gain microphone experience.

Gene returned to Tulsa and for a while hosted his own show for free on station KVOO, but within a few months was performing on the WLS Barn Dance in Chicago. There he gained the necessary experience, considerably broadened his repertoire, and was a runaway success. He also started writing his own material. When he went back to New York in 1930, ARC were the first to record him. But much of his early success on records he owed to Sears Roebuck, which had its own record label. His songs on this label were promoted through the Sears-owned WLS Barn Dance and were featured prominently in the omnipresent Sears catalog. Au-

try fans could also find advertised in that same publication the Gene Autry 'Roundup' guitar and the Gene Autry Songbook – all highly convenient.

One of Gene's first songs, which he co-wrote with Jimmy Long, was *That Silver-Haired Daddy of Mine*. Within months it had soared to the equivalent of today's No 1 spot and eventually sold in the millions. By 1934 Oklahoma's Yodeling Cowboy, as he was then known, was a household word in rural areas throughout the nation. But in the big cities few had heard of him. This was another snag that raised doubts and eyebrows among Hollywood's movie moguls when seeking a replacement for John Wayne. But the proposed B Westerns were not intended primarily for the city slickers. They would be shown precisely where Gene had his hosts of followers and where his records were bringing in cash by the truckload – in smalltown America. And that was the deciding factor.

A start in Hollywood

Gene's movie debut was in a Ken Maynard western, *In Old Santa Fe*, where his appearance was limited to a 10-minute singing spot. The response was gratifying. But he still couldn't act, and prompt steps were taken at Republic to remedy that failing. His first solo role was in *Phantom Empire*, a 12-part serial in which Gene astonishingly appeared as Gene Autry, a famous radio personality battling against the forces of evil in an absurd early sci-fi plot. As a result of this astute 12-week exposure, Gene's ratings soared.

His next film was *Tumbling Tumbleweeds*, the first movie in which he was the acknowledged star. It also provided him with another million-selling hit record in the shape of the title tune. From then on, the western *was* Gene Autry, with his equally famous horse, Champion. In the 1930s and early 1940s he was the undisputed king of the B movie.

All this time his records were selling in terrifying numbers. Among the most popular were *Yellow Rose of Texas* (1933), *The Last Roundup* (1934),

Gene Autry ran a California-based radio show, Melody Ranch, which ran for some 17 years. Its success was based on a dependable formula of music and comedy, interspersed with sketches featuring Autry and his famous horse Champion. Autry's broadcasting and recording career was interrupted by World War II, during which he served with distinction as a pilot in North Africa and the Far East with Air Transport Command.

Tumbling Tumbleweeds (1935), *Mexicali Rose* (1936), *South of the Border* (1940), and *You Are My Sunshine* (1941). Largely due to Gene's influence, country music began to acquire a new image. The old hillbilly reach-me-downs with scuffed shoes and patched pants gave way to spotless stetsons and immaculate white starched cowboy suits favored by Gene himself. And although there was little change in the music and its instruments, the lyrics were transmogrified. Traditional songs, which dealt with rivers and mountains and valleys and indolent farmers were replaced by ditties manufactured by professional scribblers in Tin Pan Alley. These described imaginatively but convincingly the rigors of the purple plains and the sameness of acres of sagebrush. These songs related intimately to the far southwest, and they put the *western* into country and western.

With Gene's bank balance now beginning to look like Fort Knox in miniature, it is not surprising that a host of imitators sprang up. The quickest way to become a millionaire, it seemed, was to list yourself as a singing cowboy. Imitators proliferated, but there was only one rival – Roy Rogers (and more of him later). Among the less successful were Bob Baker, whose movies let him down; Jack Randell, a good actor with a lousy voice, and Dick Foran, who could sing but whose acting left much to be desired.

In 1938, Gene refused to renew his contract with Republic unless they were prepared to give him a larger slice of the financial cake. They were not prepared, and defiantly signed up Roy Rogers to take his place. A discomfited Gene Autry stayed out for a while but eventually returned to the Republic fold.

Just before World War II Gene reached the peak of his fame – and what a peak it was. On his visit to Ireland, Dublin's streets were packed with a million people who turned out to welcome him. And in 1941 Berwyn, Oklahoma, paid him the signal honor of changing its name to Gene Autry, Oklahoma.

During the war Gene Autry saw distinguished service in the Middle and Far East, flying cargo and supply planes over enemy territory while in the Army Air Corps.

After the war, Gene shrewdly invested his millions in a chain of radio and TV stations, in oil, hotels, real estate, a recording company, and part ownership of a baseball team – the California Angels. As a result, his millions were converted into multi-millions, and he is today one of the wealthiest personalities in showbiz. In spite of all this activity, he still had time to record some more million-sellers for Columbia. Among his hits were *Peter Cottontail*, *Frosty Snowman*, and *Rudolph the Red-Nosed Reindeer*. *Rudolph* to date has sold more than 10 million copies and is still in great demand as each Christmas comes round.

After a career in which he had starred in more than 100 movies and produced 91 TV movies, it was only fitting that Gene Autry should be honored by being elected to the Country Music Hall of Fame in 1969.

Along came Roy Rogers

Gene Autry's illustrious career was seriously threatened by only one man – Roy Rogers. Rogers really took over where Autry left off, and although they shared the title of King of the Cowboys, bestowed on each of them by their respective fans, it is true to say that Rogers never had quite the colossal impact of his predecessor.

Tex Ritter followed Gene Autry into the movies as a singing cowboy. Although he made more than 50 films, he was quite different from Autry. His singing lacked smoothness and was sometimes off key, but he made up for this with unusual and attractive phrasing and a patent honesty of purpose that came through to his audience. His knowledge of western lore was extensive, leading many people to believe that he was a genuine cowboy.

Roy Rogers was born Leonard Slye in Cincinnati, Ohio. Raised on a farm in Portsmouth, Ohio, Roy was musically influenced from his earliest years by his mandolin- and guitar-playing father. During the 1920s he worked in a local shoe factory and filled in his spare time singing and playing at concerts and dances.

In 1930 he hitched his way to California where he earned a precarious living as a peach picker and truck driver. Under the name of Dick Weston he joined a number of Western groups such as the Rocky Mountaineers, The International Cowboys, The Hollywood Hillbillies, and The Texas Outlaws. He eventually became lead singer with The Pioneer Trio, along with Bob Nolan and Tim Spencer. The group soon established a reputation for their treatment of Western ballads and then began to gain bit parts in Western films. In 1934, when filming with Gene Autry, they changed their name to Sons of the Pioneers, and Dick Weston finally and permanently became Roy Rogers.

When Gene Autry walked out of the Republic studios in 1938 on a one-man strike, Herbert J Yates, then head of the organization, refused to be blackmailed by his erstwhile star and cast around for a replacement. He found it in Roy Rogers, who somewhat fortuitously had just been auditioned in response to an ad for a new singing cowboy. He seemed to fit the bill perfectly and Yates, still fuming over the Autry defection, lavished all the care and expense he could on his new protégé. Roy was given his first starring role in *Under Western Skies* and became an instant success. Following in the Autry tradition, he appeared with his horse Trigger, and in many movies romanced with his attractive co-star, Dale Evans. They were married in 1947.

Between 1938 and 1953 Roy Rogers starred in more than 100 movies, and from 1952 to 1954 appeared in his own TV show. Apart from his films, Roy made many recordings for Victor. Yet in spite of a good voice and a convincing yodel, none of his songs really took off in the Autry manner. Perhaps

the best known of his recordings was a novelty number, *A Four-Legged Friend*. In later years he and Dale, both committed Christians, concentrated on religious duets.

Texas cowboy lore

The only other signing cowboy to make an indelible mark on the country music scene was Tex Ritter. Woodward Maurice Ritter (he acquired the name Tex when appearing in stage plays in New York) was probably the most authentic of all the singing cowboys. He never worked as a cowboy, but his research into the history of that legendary figure, his knowledge, sincerity, and utter lack of sophistication when singing unmusically the songs he loved, separated him from all the cowboy balladeers and matinée idols who crooned Hollywood lyrics to order. Sadly, it was this very authenticity that worked against him to an extent. Although his records sold well, many preferred the smoother, slicker Tin Pan Alley version of the Wild West.

Born in Paola County, Texas, Tex Ritter was originally headed for a career in law. With that in mind, he attended the University of Texas and later spent a year at Northwestern, before deciding that it was not for him. In order to broaden his Texas horizon he traveled east to New York, and there his unmistakable Texas drawl and immense cowboy lore caused quite an impression among those who heard him. They thought he must be the genuine article, and Tex did his best to live up to it. He was offered bit parts on stage, singing western songs. In the early 1930s he appeared in a number of plays, the most important being *Green Grow the Lilacs* in which he took the lead. (This later became the basis for the musical *Oklahoma*). Tex also found himself in demand on radio, in particular on station WINS with a children's program called Cowboy Tom's Roundup and on WHN in Tex Ritter's Campfire.

Tex's career in the movies as a singing cowboy was prolific but undistinguished. During his nine years' work in

Hollywood, starting with *Song of the Gringo* in 1936, he appeared in nearly 60 films, many with his beloved horse White Flash. When it was time to quit the movies, he embarked on a punishing schedule of personal appearances throughout the nation and abroad, clocking up thousands of miles each year.

When it came to making records, Tex began with Decca as inauspiciously as he had in Hollywood. But in 1942 the newly hatched Capitol company signed him as their first country artist, and from then he never looked back. During the 1940s and 1950s he had few rivals in record sales. Among the all-time favorites were *Jingle, Jangle, Jingle* (1942), *Jealous Heart* (1944), *Rye Whiskey* (1945), *The Wayward Wind* (1956), and *I Dreamed of a Hillbilly Heaven* (1961). But perhaps his most famous contribution to the country music repertoire was his treatment of the theme song for the movie *High Noon*, which won him an Academy Award in 1953. From 1953 to 1960 he co-hosted the Los Angeles TV show Town Hall Party with Johnny Bond, thus remaining well in the public eye and esteem.

Always interested in politics, Tex ran for governor of Tennessee and failed. He was also unsuccessful in his attempt to enter the US Senate in 1970. Earlier he had helped to found the Country Music Foundation as well as the Country Music Hall of Fame. In 1964 he had his reward by being elected to the latter august body. He returned to Nashville in 1965 and joined the Grand Ole Opry. He died of a heart attack in 1974 while endeavoring to bail out one of his band members from a Nashville jail.

The new breed does well

Inevitably, the success stories of Messrs Autry, Rogers, and Ritter inspired a flood of imitators who beseiged Hollywood for the chance of appearing in some of the many B Westerns that hit the screens during and just after the Depression. A few of them made it to the top. After hearing the Wakely Trio on one of his trips, Gene Autry had invited them to meet him in California. The three lads from Oklahoma – Jimmy Wakely, Johnny

Ken Maynard serenades the lady in the film The Wagon Master, *in 1930. In so doing, he became the first cowboy to sing on film. Before that he had starred in many silent movies. Maynard was later responsible for introducing Gene Autry to films, the latter making his debut in* In Old Santa Fe *(1934).*

Bond, and Scotty Harrel – took the great man at his word and soon they had joined him on his CBS radio show The Melody Ranch Show. So popular did they become that both Wakely and Bond decided individually to seek greener pastures within two years of arriving in California.

Jimmy Wakely, from Arkansas, had based his musical style on that of Autry himself. When he left The Melody Ranch Show, Wakely formed his own band and became part of the Los Angeles County Barn Dance. Some of the characters in his group later built up formidable reputations of their own. They included Merle Travis, Spade Cooley, and the versatile Cliffie Stone. As Wakely's popularity soared, he employed his own backing group, The Saddle Pals, and over the years starred in about 50 movies.

He recorded his greatest hit in 1949, for Capitol. It was a Floyd Tillman duet with Margaret Whiting called *Slippin' Around*, which sold a million copies, and reached the No 1 spot. The duo knew a good thing when they sang one and followed this with *I'll Never Slip Around Again* and similar vocal protestations – all hits. This was the start of the so-called 'cheatin' song' boom. In spite of a number of solo successes (*My Heart Cries for You, Beautiful Brown Eyes*), Wakely gradually faded from the scene in the 1950s, his decline coinciding with the demise of the singing cowboy era.

Johnny Bond went on to record for Columbia and stayed with them for 14 years. Guitarist and singer (he accompanied Gene Autry on many of his songs in B Westerns), Bond developed into a highly acclaimed composer. Among the 500-odd numbers written by him were such hits as *Cimarron, Gone and Left Me Blues*, and *Tomorrow Never Comes*. In 1960 he recorded *Hot Rod Lincoln* for Republic and made the Top 30 in the pop charts. Bond also tasted the fruits of authorship with his autobiography and *The Tex Ritter Story*. He died of a heart attack in 1978, working almost to the end.

The last of the singing cowboys on screen was Rex Allen, the Arizona Cowboy. He came late to the movies –

Rex Allen, the Arizona Cowboy, was originally a rodeo rider. He was the last of the singing cowboys to appear on screen, in the 1950s. In 1951 he ran his own Hollywood radio show. Among his recorded hits the two most popular were Crying in the Chapel *and* Don't Go Near the Indians.

1950 – just when that breed of entertainer had reached his last gasp. Nevertheless, he featured in 32 B Westerns for Republic before doffing his stetson. Rodeo rider, singer, guitarist and fiddler, Allen opted out of a degree course in electronics and eventually settled for a showbiz career. During the 1940s he gained radio experience in Trenton, New Jersey, and became well known on the National Barn Dance. He headed his own Hollywood radio show (CBS) in 1951 and subsequently was heard singing and narrating in several Walt Disney productions. His version of *Crying in the Chapel* (1953) won him a gold disc, and nearly 10 years later he came up with a pop-oriented hit, *Don't Go Near the Indians*.

The era of western swing

Another kind of western music, allied to hillbilly but far removed from it, is western swing. This was born in western Texas, and is a fusion of country, folk, jazz, blues, and pop. It is essentially music to dance to but often carries a vocal line as well. In the late 1930s and 1940s, rural dance halls were crammed to suffocation with frenzied fans, many of whom traveled many miles to dance to the new sound.

A pioneer and the greatest exponent of western swing was Bob Wills, a versatile fiddler from Limestone County, Texas. The first of 10 children, he had tried his hand at most things – rodeo riding, preaching, cotton-picking, shacking up with outlaws – before taking up music professionally. In 1929 he and guitarist Herman Arnspiger formed a duo at Fort Worth, calling themselves The Wills Fiddle Band. A year later, Bob expanded the band to include vocalist Milton Brown, a pianist, another guitarist and a jazz banjoist. Under the sponsorship of Birrus Mills, a flour firm, they archly named themselves The Light Crust Doughboys.

In spite of great popularity on radio and on record, the band soon began to disintegrate. Milton Brown left first to form the Musical Brownies, whose swing and pop style, featuring steel guitar, made it one of the most excit-

Below and facing page: *Roy Rogers, known by his admiring fans as King of the Cowboys, was Gene Autry's only serious rival in that department. He starred in more than 100 films over a period of some 15 years. His horse, Trigger, appeared in most of them, as did his female lead, Dale Evans, whom he married in* 1947. *Rogers early formed his own band, the International Cowboys, but later he came up with a much more successful outfit, the Sons of the Pioneers, which also included such notables as Bob Nolan and Tim Spencer. Their biggest hits were* Tumbling Tumbleweeds *and* Cool Water, *both composed by Bob Nolan.*

Roy Rogers and The Cactus Cowboys

REPUBLIC PICTURES

ROY ROGERS • TRIGGER
"King of the Cowboys"   "Smartest Horse in the Movies"
"SUNSET IN THE WEST" U
with **ESTELITA RODRIGUEZ** and **PENNY EDWARDS**
GORDON JONES · WILL WRIGHT · PIERRE WATKIN
and **FOY WILLING** and the **RIDERS** of the **PURPLE SAGE**

To Bobby
Best Wishes
Roy Rogers
Trigger

ing bands around at that time. Tragically, at the peak of his popularity, Brown died in his wrecked car in 1936. His place in the Light Crust Doughboys was taken by blues singer Tommy Duncan.

Wills abandoned the outfit in late 1933, taking with him singer Tommy Duncan (country music's first crooner) and his brother Johnie Lee, who played banjo. Together with two others they moved first to Waco and then to Tulsa, Oklahoma, where they called themselves Bob Wills and his Texas Playboys. From that date they broadcast their hot dance music for some 24 years over station KVOO. In 1940 the band recorded a million-seller in *San Antonio Rose*, written by Wills for the honeyed voice of Tommy Duncan. Wills had already recorded the tune as an instrumental number two years earlier. It sold even more millions some time later when Bing Crosby turned his attention to it.

Bob Wills reached his peak in the 1930s and early 1940s. After the war, with most of the time spent in California, he was increasingly plagued by ill health. Public taste had also changed, and there was less interest in western swing. He suffered a series of heart attacks, the first striking him in 1962,

and after 1964 his touring days came to an end and his public appearances were strictly limited. In 1968, he was elected to the Country Music Hall of Fame, after making well over 500 recordings during his career.

In 1972 he was still trying to make a comeback, with a resurgence of interest in his beloved music, although he was by then confined to a wheelchair. In 1973 he attended his last recording session. He suffered a stroke on the first day and lapsed into a coma from which he never recovered, dying some 17 months later.

Among other characters who helped to spread the gospel of western swing, easily the most prominent was Spade Cooley, (he earned his nickname from a freak run of spades enjoyed in a card game), who at one time was so popular that he dared to share with Bob Wills the title of King of Western Swing. He was born in Oklahoma and became an exceptional fiddler (he earned his first professional fee on the instrument playing for square dances at the age of eight). He played several minor movie roles in the 1930s, and gradually built a band of expert musicians around him – at one time as many as 24. They specialized in jazzy dance music and were

Facing page: Roy Rogers had trained his intelligent horse Trigger to do many tricks. This flair was put to good effect in the movies, when hero Roy inevitably found himself in trouble and Trigger happily galloped to the rescue in the nick of time.

Below: Dale Evans first starred in a movie with Roy Rogers, her husband-to-be, in 1944 in a typical Western, The Cowboy and the Señorita. *From them on, she shared the limelight with him, and his horse Trigger, in dozens of similar films. Roy was an acceptable singer with a convincing yodel, but his recording career came nowhere near to matching his movie success.*

Above: *Spade Cooley, known as the King of Western Swing, appeared on stage backed by very large bands, his motto apparently being, the more the better. He derived his name from a poker game in his early days in which he found himself holding a freak run of spades.*

radio favorites for some years in the 1940s. Cooley wrote his own greatest hit, *Shame on You*, in 1945. He looked set to scale even greater heights when his career was rudely interrupted by a jail sentence for wife-slaying. In 1969, shortly after his release, he succumbed to a fatal heart attack.

There were many others who helped to popularize western swing. They included Wills' brother, Johnnie Lee, Bill Boyd and the Cowboy Ramblers, and Leon McAuliffe, who headed the Cimarron Boys and picked up the gauntlet where Wills had dropped it, resurrecting that neglected style successfully in the 1970s.

This is honky tonk

A direct offspring of western swing came to be known as honky tonk. It was a rougher, tougher type of country music spawned in the sprawling taverns and saloons of Texas. In such surroundings performers were faced with boisterous dancing, fights, drunken heckling and other unlooked for interruptions. As a result, and mostly in self-defense, musicians relied increasingly on a solid heavy beat and the aid of electrified instruments, merely to make themselves heard above the hubbub.

Lyrics, too, took on a more realistic tone. Gone were the rather dreamy, romantic tales of unrequited love and forgiving couples. In their place came harsh verses dealing with problems of the day – drink, domestic tragedies, slipping around. Honky tonk was a Texas phenomenon and most of its great names were Texans. Several of them came out of a popular swing band of the 1930s, the Blue Ridge Playboys.

Hawaiian guitarist Ted Daffan played steel with the Blue Ridge Playboys before he left them to form Ted Daffan's Texans. His *Truck Drivers' Blues*, which he wrote in 1939 and which was recorded by Decca, is alleged to be the first ever trucking song. This huge success was followed a year later by *Worried Mind*, another hit, this time for Columbia. After the war he had a double-sided triumph with *No Letter Today* and *Born to Lose*, which sold a million and earned Daffan a gold disc. His prolific pen earned him more hits in the 1950s and 1960s with offerings such as *I'm a Fool to Care, Heading Down the Wrong Highway*, and *Blue Steel Blues*.

Another honky tonk artist to emerge from the Blue Ridge Playboys was two-finger pianist Aubrey 'Moon' Mullican. The King of the Hillbilly Piano Players had a distinctive and versatile piano style that employed two fingers of the right hand to accompany his bluesy singing. He toured with many topliners, including Red Foley, Hank Williams, and Tennessee Ernie Ford, among others, and his influence can be heard in the playing of many later rockabilly piano players. He was also a songwriter of note, whose hits included *Cherokee Boogie, Jambalaya*, and the Cajun-flavored *Jole Blon*. Mullican died of a heart attack in 1967.

Multi-instrumentalist Floyd Tillman (guitar, banjo, and mandolin), another escapee from the Blue Ridge Playboys, is best known for the many honky tonk hits he wrote. Hailing originally from Oklahoma, he became hooked on Jimmie Rodgers' songs while working as a Western Union messenger boy. His greatest hit was unquestionably *Slippin' Around* (1949), which was boosted by duetists Jimmy Wakely and Margaret Whiting. But there were many other winners, too, including *It Makes No Difference Now, I Love You So Much It Hurts*, and *It Just Tore Me Up*.

Al Dexter (born Albert Poindexter), honky tonk and country blues writer and singer, was born in Jacksonville, Texas. He eventually came to head a popular band called the Texas Troupers. But he is best remembered for his *Pistol Packin' Mama*, which was released by Columbia in 1943 and later snapped up by Bing Crosby. Within two years, more than three million singles were sold. Other hits for Dexter included *Jelly Roll Blues, Honky Tonk Blues*, and *Rosalita*.

Honky tonk hero

The greatest of all the honky tonk exponents was Ernest Dale Tubb, the

Texas Troubadour. He was born at Crisp, Texas, and as a boy, along with so many others, idolized and tried to imitate Jimmie Rodgers. His imitations were dismal failures apparently, but by 1934 he had managed to get a singing spot on radio KONO, San Antonio. His lucky break came the following year when he met and was befriended by Carrie, Jimmy Rodgers' widow. She not only presented him with her late husband's prized 000-45 Martin guitar, but also decided to help him in his career. Largely through her influence he was able to record *The Passing of Jimmie Rodgers* and *Jimmie Rodgers' Last Thoughts*, released by RCA in 1936. After sponsorship by the makers of Gold Chain flour (thus accounting for his earlier nickname of the Gold Chain Troubadour), and a few bit parts in the movies, he penned his first big hit in 1942, *Walking the Floor Over You*. This runaway success helped to ensure his membership of the Grand Ole Opry in 1943.

In 1947 Tubb opened his world famous record shop in Nashville, whose wares he advertised in his Midnight Jamboree program over WSM. From the early 1950s onwards he figured prominently in the hit list with numbers such as *Missing in Action*, *Goodnight Irene*, and *Another Story, Another Time, Another Place*. Many of his recorded successes featured duets with other stars such as Red Foley, the Andrews Sisters, and Loretta Lynn.

Ernest Tubb was elected to the Country Music Hall of Fame in 1965, the sixth individual to be so honored. He had an itchy foot, traveling more than 100,000 miles each year and never seeming to stay too long in one place. His unflagging and genuine popularity has been a source of wonder to some critics. His grating and frequently off-key voice, accompanied by electric guitar (he was one of the first regularly to use this instrument), was hardly an asset. Perhaps it was his warmth, sincerity, and uncomplicated honky tonk approach that appealed to so many millions for so many years. Tubb's remarkable energy finally gave out, and he died in 1984.

4 Bluegrass, Gospel and Cajun

Facing page: *The dobro is an acoustic 6-string guitar incorporating a metal resonator. It can be played in the usual way, but more often in bluegrass bands it is laid flat and the strings fretted with a glass or slide (bottleneck). The tone is amplified acoustically to resemble that of a Hawaian guitar. It was invented around 1925 by the DOpyera BROthers, and it was ingeniously thus named after them. Among dobro experts are Josh Graves and Mike Auldridge.*

Bluegrass is a form of country music that is both old and new. It was originally presented in more or less its standard form by Bill Monroe and his Blue Grass Boys at the Grand Ole Opry in the early 1940s. Monroe, who came from the Blue Grass State of Kentucky, coined the name of his band and, by extension, of its unique sound.

Bluegrass evolved from the line-up and sounds of the old string bands, and in its traditional form features only acoustic (unamplified) instruments. Indeed, Monroe ordained that a genuine bluegrass outfit should consist exclusively of string bass, guitar, banjo, mandolin, and fiddle. Later traditional bands relaxed these strictures to include at times dobro and/or autoharp. The 'newgrass' groups of the 1970s and 1980s, which were sometimes barely distinguishable from conventional pop rock bands, turned happily to such heretical instruments as pedal steel, electric guitars, banjos, and mandolins, as well as pianos and drums.

Unique features of bluegrass are its simple, homely, down-to-earth lyrics, the 'high and lonesome' emotional tenor voice, weaving its harmonies above the lead, and the sometimes overpowering voice of the banjo often blasting at breakneck speed to identify this 'folk music with overdrive', as it has been described. Instrumentalists take it in turn to provide individual breaks (as in traditional jazz) in between spots of solo or chorus singing, and the best of them are highly skilled musicians.

The 5-string banjo achieved its prominence with the arrival of one Earl Scruggs, whose influence on banjo-playing has been likened to that of Paganini on the violin and Segovia on the classical guitar. Scruggs joined Monroe's band in 1945 at the age of 19. His electrifying three-finger picking (developed from the earlier styles of Smith Hammed and Snuffy Jenkins) revolutionized and stamped a permanent hallmark on the sound of bluegrass. Other outstanding musicians serving with Bill Monroe at the time included vocalist and guitarist Lester Flatt, fiddler Chubby Wise, and bassist Howard Watts (Cedric Rainwater). Some bluegrass classics were recorded during that period, including *Blue Moon of Kentucky* (later taken up by Elvis Presley), *Uncle Pen*, *Walking in Jerusalem*, *Back Up and Push*, and *Orange Blossom Special*. Bill was elected to the Country Music Hall of Fame in 1970.

The Foggy Mountain Boys

In 1948 Earl Scruggs and Lester Flatt left Bill Monroe to form their own band – Flatt and Scruggs and the Foggy Mountain Boys. Lester Flatt began as a 'weekend' guitarist, his income coming from work in a Tennessee tex-

Above: *Flatt and Scruggs formed the greatest bluegrass partnership in the history of country music. Their professional association lasted 21 years, after coming out of Bill Monroe's Blue Grass Boys in 1948. Flatt was the vocalist and guitarist; Scruggs provided his unique, fast-driving 5-string banjo expertise and filled in with occasional finger-style guitar. To the worldwide dismay of bluegrass fans, they went their separate ways in 1969.*

Facing page: *The Monroe Brothers face up bravely to their fan mail. The Monroes – Birch (fiddle), Charlie (guitar), and Bill (mandolin) – worked together at manual jobs in East Chicago, Indiana, from 1929 to 1934. At night they played for parties and dances of various kinds. A break came in 1934 when Radio WLS Chicago offered them full time musical work. It was just then that Birch decided he'd had enough of music and quit. Bill and Charlie soldiered on as a duo.*

Right: *Bill Monroe, youngest and most famous of the Monroe Brothers, is known as the Father of Bluegrass. A wizard of the mandolin and possessed of a high tenor voice, he formed his own band of expert musicians – the Blue Grass Boys. Over the years he and his band brought to light and defined the unique sound of bluegrass.*

tile mill. In 1939 he started radio work from Roanoke, Virginia, and in 1944 was invited by Bill Monroe to join his outfit on the Grand Ole Opry. Lester sang tenor and filled in on guitar, but he was faced with a problem. Because of the unusual speed with which most of the numbers were taken, he found it difficult to fit all the notes in. His solution was to catch up with a little upward run of three or four notes on the lower strings, and because the tuning was generally in G, it became known in bluegrass circles as 'the Lester Flatt G run'.

When Flatt and Scruggs took their leave of Monroe (allegedly because they couldn't stand the pace of the latter's indefatigable touring), they took with them Howard Watts on bass and Jim Shumate on fiddle. They were later joined by Mac Wiseman (guitar and vocals), and almost immediately began regular radio work from Hickory, in North Carolina, and recording for Mercury.

Their vocal harmonies were smoother than Monroe's, and there was less emphasis on the mandolin (it was finally dropped altogether in favor of the dobro). In later years (they celebrated a 21-year partnership) their style became so professional, so smooth and proficient, that it seemed to lose some of that earlier verve and spontaneity. Nevertheless, it was superb musicianship by any standards. In 1949 they recorded their famous *Foggy Mountain Breakdown*, which was used to heighten the excitement of the car chase in the film *Bonnie and Clyde*.

The CBS-TV series, *The Beverley Hillbillies*, allowed them a further opportunity to provide the theme tune, this time *The Ballad of Jed Clampett*. From December 1962 it held the number one spot in the country charts for three months – the only bluegrass number ever to reach those heights. From 1953, Flatt and Scruggs were sponsored on WSM Nashville by Martha White Flour, and even the product's signature tune, as rendered by the Foggy Mountain Boys, was recorded and became a hot favorite.

Other classic recordings by the group (which eventually came to be acknowledged as the finest and most representative bluegrass outfit in the world) included *Roll in My Sweet Baby's Arms*, *Salty Dog Blues*, *Earl's Breakdown*, and *Jimmy Brown the Newsboy*. It is ironic that in the mid-1950s, after establishing themselves in the Grand Ole Opry, they were traveling all over the nation far more than they ever did with Bill Monroe, whose band they had left in order to get a rest.

In 1969 the country music world was stunned to learn that Flatt and Scruggs had decided to go their separate ways. Scruggs had been hankering to experiment with new sounds, new instrumentation, new directions. He was convinced that bluegrass had to move with the times. As a result, he formed the Earl Scruggs Revue, which consisted mainly of himself and his sons, with dobro artist Buck (Josh) Graves. Their line-up included electric bass, slide guitar, and harmonica, concentrating mostly on country rock.

Flatt preferred to stick to the more

69

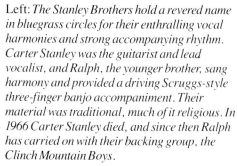

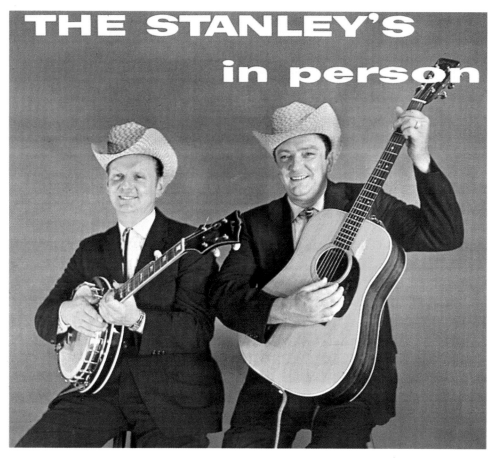

Left: *The Stanley Brothers hold a revered name in bluegrass circles for their enthralling vocal harmonies and strong accompanying rhythm. Carter Stanley was the guitarist and lead vocalist, and Ralph, the younger brother, sang harmony and provided a driving Scruggs-style three-finger banjo accompaniment. Their material was traditional, much of it religious. In 1966 Carter Stanley died, and since then Ralph has carried on with their backing group, the Clinch Mountain Boys.*

Facing page: *Lester Flatt and Earl Scruggs gained worldwide recognition outside the world of country music and bluegrass for their tingling, toe-tapping musical accompaniment to the film* Bonnie and Clyde. *After parting in 1969, Scruggs formed his own progressive group, the Earl Scruggs Revue.*

Below: *The Stanley Brothers were raised on oldtime mountain music and this was reflected throughout their professional careers. Carter composed most of their songs, which they performed with a modern touch but with evident reverence for tradition. Among their hits were* White Dove, Lonesome River, *and* Dream of the Miner's Child.

traditional style, retaining most of the Foggy Mountain Boys in his newly formed Nashville Grass, and later teaming up once more with his former partner, Mac Wiseman.

Another great bluegrass duo were the Stanley Brothers. Originally forming an old-time band, The Clinch Mountain Boys, in 1946, they began by broadcasting from Bristol, Virginia. Eventually they changed direction from old timey to bluegrass and gospel. In 1948 they caused a sensation with their recording of *Molly and the Tenbrooks*. From then on, into the 1950s and 1960s, their recordings for Columbia, Mercury, Starday, and King won them an ardent following among bluegrass and gospel aficionados alike.

The brothers were born in Virginia. Carter, the elder, was lead vocalist and guitarist; Ralph played superb banjo Scruggs-style. They were backed by a variety of bass, fiddle, and mandolin players at different times, and their harmonies were rated as some of the most inspiring sounds in country music. In 1955 they were voted The Best Instrumental Group. Among

Jim and Jesse McReynolds, a famous bluegrass duo, owe much to the superb mandolin playing of Jesse. He developed his unique style by patterning the bluegrass banjoist's finger-picking technique and adapting it to the mandolin with flat pick. Jim's high tenor vocalizing lends the partnership a more modern Nashville sound. The brothers made their first professional impact in the early 1960s and were still going very strong and delighting audiences in the mid-1980s with numbers such as Snowbird.

their all-time greats were *Little Glass of Wine, Pretty Polly, Train 45*, and *Midnight Ramble*. Carter Stanley died in 1966, but Ralph continued the tradition with the Clinch Mountain Boys, releasing a notable album *In Memory of Carter Stanley*, made up mostly of gospel numbers.

Bluegrass through to the eighties

A favorite and influential bluegrass duo were brothers Jim and Jesse McReynolds, from Coeburn, Virginia. They were first heard on radio in 1947, and were very much alive and performing to great acclaim all over the world almost 40 years later. It was these live performances that established them firmly in the bluegrass hierarchy, their records strangely making little impact. Jim's guitar, together with Jesse's unusual cross-picking on mandolin and close vocal harmonies, backed by their band The Virginia Boys, have delighted audiences at the Grand Old Opry since 1964.

The Country Gentlemen came up with quite a different face of bluegrass for their insatiable fans. The original group was made up of Charlie Waller (guitar), John Duffey (tenor and mandolin), Eddie Adcock (banjo), and Tom Grey (bass). Waller's solid rhythm. Duffey's high lead tenor and mesmerizing fingers flying all over the mandolin, and Adcock's jazzy mastery of the banjo combined to produce sounds previously unheard from a bluegrass band. They were equally at home with traditional ballads, calypso, and jazz, and working out of Washington, DC, they became outstandingly popular with a wide variety of audiences at bluegrass festivals, coffee-houses, and colleges throughout the nation. Among their many recordings they produced versions of *Bringing Mary Home, Letter to Tom, The Fields Have Turned Brown*, and *Poor Ellen Smith*.

Left and above: *Bill Clifton, bluegrass and old-time exponent, has taken his talents and love of music to many parts of the world. Guitarist, autoharp expert, and singer, he has done much to popularize American traditional music in Europe (especially in England) and in the Far East and Australasia. Meticulous in his performances, both live and recorded, he managed to surround himself with backing musicians of the highest caliber. On any one of Bill's discs you can see names such as Mike Seeger, Ralph Stanley, John Duffey, Benny Martin, and others who together with Bill's own talented group, the Dixie Mountain Boys, contribute to unforgettable performances. In additon to his musical activities, in which he draws heavily on Carter Family material, Bill is a graduate engineer, and ex-marine officer, and a director of the Peace Corps. He has co-ordinated one of the Newport Folk Festivals and laid on tours abroad for bluegrass artists.*

From a strictly bluegrass standpoint, the Osborne Brothers carry a somewhat tarnished reputation with the purists because of their free use of electrified instruments, drums, and piano. Bob and Sonny Osborne were born at Hyden, Kentucky in the 1930s and were not heard on radio until the early 1950s. As they became better known, they did a stint with Jimmy Martin, and then in 1959 they formed a trio with guitarist Benny Birchfield. With Bob on mandolin and fiddle, and Sonny on banjo and guitar, they developed a razor-sharp, nerve-tingling three-part vocal harmony – Sonny's baritone, Bob's soaring tenor, and Benny filling in the spaces in between.

That same year they appeared at Antioch College (which opened up for them an unending series of campus dates) and in doing so became the first bluegrass outfit to play college dates. In 1963 they ended a seven-year connection with MGM and signed for Decca. A year after that they were accepted as regular members of the Grand Ole Opry. In 1973 they registered another first by appearing with Merle Haggard at the prestigious Harrah's Club, Lake Tahoe, Nevada, where no bluegrass band had played before.

From the early 1970s the group enraged dyed-in-the-wool traditionalists by plugging their instruments into the mains, including an electrified dobro and pedal steel. Their excuse at the time was that their acoustic strings were being swamped noisewise by the amplified groups that they shared the stage with. This switch in attitude may have lost them some of the faithful but it brought them a much wider audience from swell nightclubs, exclusive hotels, and even included an invitation from the White House. Out of many hits their two most outstanding were *Rocky Top* and *Midnight Flyer*.

Bill Clifton was largely responsible for popularizing country music, and especially bluegrass, in Britain and other parts of Europe. An ex-Marine officer with a Master's degree, Bill came from the Blue Ridge Mountains and made his professional debut with his Dixie Mountain Boys in the 1950s. His unaffected and pleasing guitar style, effective autoharp, and clear, resonant voice combined ideally to put over his favorite ballad and 'story' songs. Midway through his career, Bill opted to tote his wife and seven children to England where he made his home for several years. There he spread the good news of bluegrass, and many flourishing British bluegrass centers owe their genesis to his influence. All his life a fervent admirer of the Carter Family, Bill has recorded many of their standards, in addition to much traditional mountain music. In these he has sometimes had the co-operation of other illustrious performers such as Mike Seeger, Smiley Hobbs, Ralph Stanley, John Duffey, Red Rector, and Benny Martin. Their waxings included such classics as *Green Fields of Virginia*, *My Clinch Mountain Home*, *Dixie Darling*, and *Old Cottage Home*.

The Kentucky Colonels

Their many admirers claim that the

75

Kentucky Colonels were unquestionably the finest bluegrass ensemble ever. The band consisted of brothers Clarence (who played rhythm and lead guitar and sang lead and baritone) and Roland White (who played mandolin and sang lead and tenor), Roger Bush (who played bass and sang lead), and Billy Ray (who played banjo and sang high lead, tenor, and high baritone). This blend of superb vocal harmonies and tasteful instrumental virtuosity appealed to musicians of widely varying tastes from folkniks to rock fans. Clarence White was arguably (with a bow to Doc Watson) the finest flatpick guitarist ever, and even his partners could hardly believe what they were seeing and hearing once he launched into one of his dazzling yet perfectly controlled runs. Innovative mandolin picking from Roland and an awesome progressive banjo technique contributed by Billy Ray could be enjoyed in a repertoire that ranged from traditional numbers such as *Shuckin' the Corn* to an offbeat, Django-like treatment of *Sheik of Araby*. In 1973 Clarence was tragically knocked down and killed by a drunken car driver.

Bluegrass growing wild

There have been other bluegrass stalwarts down the years. Tennessee guitarist Jimmy Martin was lead singer for Bill Monroe from 1949 to 1953. He later formed his own band, the Sunny Mountain Boys, and cut some notable tracks for Decca. Known for gathering round him musicians of the highest quality, such as Vic Jordan, Allan Munde, and J D Crowe, he has been nevertheless frowned upon by traditionalists for introducing drums into his outfit.

The Greenbriar boys were a young, lively bluegrass group formed in 1958 and based in New York. They were formed by guitarist and tenor John Herald, tenor and banjo-contest winner Bob Yellin, and banjoist Eric Weissberg. With later changes of personnel, they included mandolinist Frank Wakefield, and musicologist, baritone and mandolinist Ralph Rinzler. They won the Old-Time Band Competition at the Fiddlers' Convention in Union Grove, North Carolina, in 1960, and charmed audiences of the folk and bluegrass circuits with their warm-hearted, good-natured expertise. They recorded a variety of tracks for Elektra and Vanguard, ranging from old Riley Puckett songs such as *Sleepy-Eyed John* to Yellin compositions, for example, *A Minor Breakdown*.

The Dillards was a group formed by four lads from Missouri who later moved to the West Coast. They were brothers Douglas and Rodney Dillard, and friends Dean Webb and Mitchell Jayne. The Dillard brothers, magnificent multi-instrumentalists, claimed to have 32 banjo-pickers and many fiddlers and guitarists in their immediate ancestry. Within the group, Doug concentrated on banjo ('the fastest banjo in the West') and Rodney on guitar and dobro. Dean Webb could also play anything with strings but specialized in the mandolin. Jayne was the group's spokesman and bass player. The Dillards played largely traditional material such as *Reuben's Train* and the old fiddle tune *Lonesome Indian*, together with compositions of their own in the mountain genre. They were well received, especially by younger audiences, who welcomed a fresh, free-ranging approach to familiar material. In 1968 they produced an album called *Wheatstraw Suite* which marked an unmistakable change in their orientation. Rodney had left the group and been replaced by Herb Pedersen (a country-rock musician from Los Angeles) and Tim Hardin. Their more commercial, rock-slanted approach included songs by Hardin and Lennon and McCartney.

Reno and Smiley and the Tennessee Cutups are more names to conjure with in the bluegrass world. Banjoist Don Reno found himself in harness

Facing page: *Country Gazette was an uptempo bluegrass outfit that was formed out of the remains of the California-based country rock band, the Flying Burrito Brothers.*

The Dillards were a talented and lighthearted group of young men who formed a band specializing in a mixture of country rock and bluegrass. In the 1960s the outfit was made up of Doug Dillard (banjo), his younger brother Rodney (guitar), Mitch Jayne, and Dean Webb. Originally hailing from Missouri, the Dillards headed for California in the 1960s where they cut some classic albums for Elektra.

from the age of 12 when he worked with the Morriss Brothers. He later collaborated with Arthur 'Guitar Boogie' Smith in their sensational million-seller, *Guitar Boogie*. He joined Bill Monroe in 1947 and left two years later to form the Tennessee Cutups. Reno teamed up with singer Red Smiley in 1950, and together they cut 16 tracks for King in 1952. After Reno and Smiley parted, Reno went back to Arthur Smith and recorded another great hit, *I'm Using My Bible for a Roadman*. Reno and Smiley came together again in 1955 and the partnership lasted for 10 years, until Smiley's health began to fail. Bill Harrell then joined Reno and they formed a new group called the Bluegrass Cutups. Reno and Smiley produced memorable recordings of tradi-

tional material and their own compositions, all backed with a solid bluegrass sound. Don Reno died of heart failure in 1984.

Country Gazette, a contemporary bluegrass band, rose Phoenix-like from the ashes of California's notorious country rock group, the Flying Burrito Brothers. The original line-up in the early 1970s consisted of award-winning fiddler Byron Berline, banjoist Alan Munde, bassist Roger Bush, Kenny Wertz, who sang and played guitar, and Roland White, late of the Kentucky Colonels, who supplied mandolin, guitar and vocals. Their slick, modern style, both instrumental and vocal, was applied to traditional material and self-penned compositions, interlaced with broad farce. Perhaps because of increasingly stiff

competition in that field, their national success was limited, but their popularity in Europe, and especially in England, won them many awards. The makeup of the band has changed several times in the last few years.

The country gospel tradition

Closely allied to bluegrass, and in many ways forming a part of it, has been country gospel music. It stemmed originally from the singing conventions of the 19th century which were held at regular intervals in churches or public meeting places in the south. The quiet, earnest, sedate hymns that had been brought to America from the Protestant churches of Europe were modified and adapted to suit the more primitive and livelier settings of the New World. Books of sacred songs were later printed with

shaped notes to indicate pitch. *The Sacred Harp*, first published in 1844, was a highly popular collection of such songs, and is still used today.

Towards the end of the 1900s, gospel music began to feel the taint of commercialism with the enormous revival meetings run by Moody and Sankey and the songbooks they sponsored. Songs became excessively sentimental and introspective, with titles such as *Where We'll Never Grow Old*, *Mother's Not Dead*, and *The Drunkard's Child*, which could always move an audience to tears. Many of today's classics, such as *Amazing Grace*, *Heavenly Sunlight*, and *'Tis the Old Time Religion*, were written at the turn of the century and have been recorded by dozens of gospel and country bands.

The Dillards' approach to bluegrass was progressive and experimental, and their use of electrified instruments disgusted some traditional fans but gained them a large new following among the younger generation. Two of their earlier popular recordings were Back Porch Bluegrass *and* Live! Almost! *Doug Dillard eventually left the group and after working with the Byrds, went solo.*

79

At that time, too, sacred songs began to be promulgated by means of vocal quartets. From these evolved some of the best known gospel groups in country music, and their smooth harmonies set the pattern for much secular country music. In addition to group singing, many of the solo country music stars of later years graduated from the hymn-singing days of their youth. Among these were A P Carter, Tennessee Ernie Ford, and Lester Flatt. One of the most influential gospel groups was the Chuck Wagon Gang, who first saw the light in the 1930s. Where the traditional gospel quartet usually managed with voices and piano, the Gang preferred to use guitars, mandolins and other stringed instruments, revealing their folk and country roots. They operated mainly in the Fort Worth area of Texas, and were made up of father D P Carter, and children Ernest, Rose, and Anna.

Many bluegrass groups, who perhaps made their name from performances of secular numbers, felt it obligatory to record at least one album of sacred songs, sometimes maybe from a genuinely religious motive, at other times perhaps as a sop to the commercial interests involved. Among these were Flatt and Scruggs, the Stanley Brothers (whose output was very largely made up of gospel music), and the Louvin Brothers.

Charlie and Ira Louvin built their reputation on their magnificent close harmony vocals. Born in Alabama and raised on a farm, they sang in church and learnt to play guitar as young lads. While still in their teens they turned to writing songs of their own, religious themes being their chief inspiration. Their careers were interrupted by war service (World War II and Korea). In the 1950s they signed for MGM and Capitol, and soon they were appearing regularly on the Opry.

In the early 1960s the Louvin brothers separated, and in 1965 Ira and his wife were killed in a head-on car crash. Charlie carried on as a solo artist, appeared in the movies, and recorded some successful duets with Melba Montgomery. An inspirational release of gospel numbers by the Louvin Brothers (all self-penned save one) was titled *The Family Who Prays*.

The Blackwood Brothers Quartet was a traditional gospel group formed in the 1930s in the town of Ackerman, Mississippi. The quartet was originally made up of three brothers, Roy, James, and Doyle, and Roy's son, R W. Before World War II they roamed the southern states with great success, but during the war they switched to San Diego, California, where they worked in munitions factories. By the mid-1950s only James and R W were left of the original members in the group. The gaps were made up by Bill Shaw and Bill Lyles, with Jack Mar-

Above and right: *Doug Kershaw, figurehead and popularizer of Cajun music, is known to his fans as the Ragin' Cajun. His wild fiddle playing and high pitched whoops are a feature of his performances, live and recorded. His first public appearance was at the age of eight, singing with his mother, Mama Rita, at the Bucket of Blood, an unsavory club in Port Arthur, Louisiana. In the 1950s he and his brother Rusty recorded hits such as* Louisiana Man *and* Diggy Liggy Lo, *which effectively introduced Cajun to an international audience.*

shall on piano. Hard on the heels of a gratifying success with *The Man Upstairs* in the Arthur Godfrey talent show in New York, they were tragically bereaved by the loss of Bill Lyles and R W in a plane wreck.

More changes of personnel in the Blackwood Brothers Quartet, and more success, followed. They set themselves up in Memphis, Tennessee, and before long were acknowledged to be the most popular gospel group in the nation. Their repertoire was wide and varied, with gospel numbers old and new, and impeccably performed. Among the fans' all-time favorites were *Redemption Draweth Nigh, In the Sweet Bye and Bye,* and *Put Your Hand in the Hand.*

In the strictly bluegrass tradition, the most in-demand gospel group was undoubtedly the Lewis Family of Augusta, Georgia. They were made up of Roy 'Pop' Lewis, and his three sons, Wallace, Talmadge, and Little Roy,

together with his three daughters, Miggie, Polly, and Janis. The many members of this prolific family (Ma helped in the background with all the practical aspects of showbiz) came to be known as The First Family of Gospel Song. Their offerings were made up of hymns, gospel numbers, spirituals, and a sprinkling of their own religious compositions. Variety was sustained by a bewildering succession and combination of solos, duets, trios, quartets, quintets, and instrumentals, all highly professionally performed. Little Roy, whom Earl Scruggs once described as one of the finest banjo pickers in the land, took leads on banjo and sometimes on guitar; Talmadge took mandolin and fiddle leads; and the girls sang harmony. The Lewis family made personal appearances for many years, broadcast regularly, and recorded albums for Starday and Canaan. Among their most requested items were *Climbing Jacob's Ladder,*

Tramp on the Street, and *Leaning on the Lord*.

Cajun, the French connection

Cajun music, although a minority taste in country music, is still extremely popular in southeastern Texas and the bayou regions of Louisiana. The name is a corruption of Acadian, the original 10,000 French settlers of l'Acadie (later renamed Nova Scotia) having been deported by the victorious British in the 1700s to the Southern states of America. There, those that were not enslaved settled in French Louisiana. The music is a throwback to the folk music of the peoples of Brittany, Picardy, and Normandy, with high, plaintive singing accompanied by droning fiddles, accordions, and triangles.

The first Cajun sounds were recorded in the early 1920s and, as the music spread, various influences were absorbed – blues, jazz, western swing, string band country music, and the strong Germanic impress of the accordion. Other instruments came along too, including guitar, bass, mandolin, and even washboard, for rhythm.

The most popular of the early Cajun bands were the Hackberry Ramblers. They consisted of Luderin Darbone (leader and fiddle), Edwin Duhon (mandolin), Lennis Sonnier (guitar and vocals), Floyd Rainwater (bass), Joe Werner (guitar), and Lonnie Rainwater (guitar). They sang in English and Cajun patois, and did much to spread the popularity of their music in the 1930s. The first Cajun hit, *Jole Blon* (originally *Jolie Blonde*), was recorded in 1946 by French fiddle-player Harry Choates. Choates had a short and stormy life. Overfond of the bottle, he was slung into jail at the age of 28 for wife and child desertion, and died in 1951 within a few days of his detention.

Among later exponents of Cajun were brothers Doug and Rusty Kershaw, and Jimmy 'C' Newman. Doug Kershaw (who claims to play 28 instruments) was born in Tiel Ridge, Louisiana, with French as his mother tongue. The family moved to Lake Arthur, Louisiana, where Doug earned a meager living as a shoeshine boy and learnt to play fiddle. Accompanied by his mother Rita on guitar, he appeared occasionally at Lake Arthur's Bucket of Blood club. In their teens, Doug and Rusty began to write their own songs, and some of these were so good that they eventually led the brothers to an association with Acuff-Rose and Hickory Records in Nashville. Their growing popularity brought them regular spots

on The World's Original Jamboree in Wheeling, West Virginia, and on Shreveport's Louisiana Hayride.

It was in the early 1960s that their greatest hits were recorded. *Louisiana Man* was a Doug Kershaw original (it has since been recorded by different artists about 900 times), and *Diggy Diggy Lo* was also a sensational seller. The brothers parted in 1964, with Rusty fighting a successful war against alcoholism. Doug went on to greater heights, being invited to perform on Johnny Cash's famous TV variety show, and appearing with Bob Dylan. He has since made many live and TV appearances.

Jimmy 'C' Newman, whose ancestry was half French, was born in Mamou, Louisiana, in 1927. His original successes were based on country music with only a slight flavor of Cajun. His first hit (out of 40 or so) was

Cry, Cry Darling, in 1954. In 1956 he was appearing regularly on the Opry, and 12 months later came his biggest chart success, *A Fallen Star*. Later, Newman formed his own band, Cajun Country. His two greatest offerings in the Cajun mold were *Alligator Man* (1961) and *Boo Dan* (1969). His high-pitched screams of 'Aaa-yeee' were still thrilling audiences all the way from the US to Europe in the 1980s.

Above: *Jimmy C Newman (the C stands for Cajun) was born and raised in Bayou country and first hit the charts in 1954 with* Cry, Cry Darling. *He heads a group called Cajun Country, and their music is a shrewd meld of traditional Cajun and contemporary country.* Facing page left: *Nashville at night, but country music never sleeps.* Center: *On the fringes of bluegrass festivals there is always the opportunity to learn a new lick.*

5 **Hank and other Heroes**

Facing page: The legendary Hank Williams, singer, songwriter, and hillbilly poet, brought country music to the attention of Tin Pan Alley and did more than anyone else to enrich America's musical heritage with the songs of the people. He broke down traditional barriers between folk, country, and pop, and with his free use of steel and electric guitars, prefigured the Nashville sound.

The one man who arguably has had more influence on country music than any other was Hank Williams. Tall, gangling, uncouth, semiliterate, a man who could neither read nor write music; a man who had no great voice, and could only play a few basic chords on the guitar; and a man to whom (certainly in his later years) booze and pills were second nature – all this and more was Hank Williams. And yet he became, along with Stephen Foster perhaps, America's finest songwriter, one of the most exciting performers to hear and watch, and one who left an impress on country music that will remain forever indelible. His rise was truly meteoric, and his fall was almost as dramatic.

Born in 1923 on a rundown farm at Mount Olive, near Georgiana, Alabama, Hiram King Williams was raised almost exclusively by his dominant mother, his father being a hospitalized veteran. His mother, Lillian, was church organist, so six-year-old Hank inevitably joined the church choir. As a youngster he shone shoes and sold peanuts on street corners. A black busker called Tee-tot (Rufe Payne), whom Hank met on the streets of Georgiana and Greenville, taught him basic guitar, a feel for the blues, and how to put a song across.

At the age of 12 he wrote a song, *WPA Blues*, which easily carried the day in a songwriting contest. With $15

first prize money burning a hole in his pocket, he decided to spend it on forming his own band – the Drifting Cowboys. Basic personnel were Hilous Butrum and later Cedric Rainwater on bass, Bob McNett and later Sammy Prutett on lead guitar, Don Helms on steel guitar, and Jerry Rivers on fiddle. They were all better instrumentalists than Hank, especially Don Helms, whose steel guitar had a special affinity with Hank's 'high and lonesome' singing style.

In his late teens Hank tried a spot of rodeo riding, was thrown, and ever after suffered from a severely damaged back. During the 1940s he tried his hand at a number of jobs, including shipyard work. He and his group also broadcast occasionally from WSFA Montgomery. But he kept on writing his songs. At this time also he started a stormy courtship with Audrey Mae Sheppard, a pretty girl from southern Alabama. In the fall of 1946, 24-year-old Hank, a gaunt young man with a haunted look in his deep brown eyes, traveled to Nashville in search of a publisher for his songs. In the 10 years that he had been scribbling, not one of his songs had seen print. He approached the offices of Acuff-Rose and once inside proceeded to sing for Fred and Wesley (father and son) Rose six of his self-penned songs. It did the trick far more effectively than any manuscripts – they signed him up on

Hank Williams, a charismatic figure on stage with gaunt face and deep-set eyes, could never come to terms with his sudden wealth and popularity. He died, at 29, completely burned out, leaving behind him 125 self-penned songs, many of which brought fame and fortune to later recording artists. As his self-destructive life, tragically poisoned with pills and alcohol, neared its end, Hank's songs became increasingly despondent, pointedly forecasting his own death.

the spot. Following this, Hank recorded in the WSM studio four sides for a New York label, Sterling Records. They were *Wealth Won't Save Your Soul*, *When God Comes and Gathers His Jewels*, *My Love for You*, and *Never Again*.

Fred Rose took the recordings to New York and secured a contract with MGM Records. Very soon after he managed to get Hank on the influential Louisiana Hayride, a Saturday night show from radio KWKH, Shreveport, Louisiana. From then on Fred Rose took Hank completely under his wing, arranging and supervising the details of every recording session, producing, playing, and even adding his own touches to the songwriting.

Entry at the Opry

His success at the Hayride (although this was precarious enough when his drinking bouts began to interfere with his performances) finally earned him an appearance at the Grand Ole Opry. It was on 11th June 1949 that he made

his bow on the Opry stage. When he launched into his *Lovesick Blues* (the recording had previously been well received) the audience went berserk. After a standing ovation and six encores Hank disappeared offstage with the applause ringing in his ears for at least another five minutes. For the next three years Hank was a regular at the Opry, who put up with his frequent last-minute absenteeism and bouts of drunkenness with increasing impatience.

One prolific source of Hank's songs was his relationship with Audrey to whom he stayed married for some eight mostly unhappy years. When he was on a high with her the songs tended to be joyful, but mostly the titles reflected a situation that offered endless pickings for the gossip-writers of the time: *Your Cheatin' Heart*, *I Can't Help It (if I'm Still in Love with You)*, *Cold, Cold Heart*. All in all, Hank recorded about 125 songs, and very few of these were forgettable. Among many hits were *My Bucket's*

Got a Hole in It, *Howlin' at the Moon*, *Honky Tonk Blues* (a rueful reflection of his hard boozing, hard loving way of life), *Jambalaya*, and the prophetic *I'll Never Get Out of This World Alive*.

Hank enjoyed being rich but was far from mean (he was quite open-handed with needy friends). What he liked more than anything was popularity, and applause was meat, if not drink, to him. Rose meanwhile had a brainwave. He felt that Hank's songs, by their very simplicity and directness, would go straight to the hearts not only of country but also of pop fans. He sold the idea to the directors of Columbia Records. As a result, Hank's *Cold, Cold Heart*, recorded by Tony Bennett soared up to the top of the *pop* charts with sales of more than a million. This opened the pop floodgates: there followed Jo Stafford with *Jambalaya*, Joni James with *Your Cheatin' Heart*, Ray Charles with *Take These Chains from My Heart*, and many, many more, right up to this day. His songs were accepted eagerly not only by pop singers but also by folk singers, black artists, and rock bands. Thus it was that Hank Williams became the first to sweep away the artificial barrier that stood between country music and other kinds of popular music – his country music from then on was national music.

In the fall of 1952 Hank hit an all-time low. In spite of international recognition and money pouring in from many sources, his personal affairs were decidedly bleak. He was fired from the Opry for perpetual drunkenness, his wife divorced him, and he was racked with pain from a variety of unpleasant diseases. He wasted no time marrying again – this time to Billie Jean Jones, the daughter of a Louisiana police chief.

On New Year's Day 1953 he was being chauffeur-driven through a snow storm to a gig in Canton, Ohio, when he fell asleep on the back seat and never woke up again. The verdict was heart failure induced by excessive alcohol. Hank was just 29.

Above: *Nashville beckons alluringly to aspiring young pickers and singers, but most of them end up with dreams unfulfilled.*

Eddy
Arnold

The flame that had burnt so brightly for a brief six years had been suddenly extinguished.

Twenty thousand people attended his funeral in Montgomery, Alabama. Hank Williams, Fred Rose, and Jimmie Rodgers were the first three artists to be honored in the Country Music Hall of Fame. The year was 1961. Hank Williams' plaque reads in part: 'Hank Williams will live on in the memories of Americans. The simple, beautiful melodies and straightforward plaintive stories in his lyrics, of life as he knew it, will never die. His songs appealed not only to the country music field, but brought him great acclaim in the 'pop' music world as well'.

Eddy sings country

One of the first of the postwar country superstars who, like Hank Williams, crossed the barrier between country and pop was the Tennessee Plowboy, Eddy Arnold. By the 1980s he had sold well over 70 million discs, which makes him easily the largest-selling country artist of all time. Eddy (given names Richard Edward) was raised on a farm near Henderson, Tennessee, and was early taught guitar by his old-time fiddler father. He played and sang at local dances and school shows during the early 1930s, making his first broadcast in 1936 on Jackson radio WTJS.

In the early 1940s Eddy made regular appearances on the Grand Ole Opry as a singer/guitarist with Pee Wee King's Golden West Cowboys. In 1944 he signed for RCA and, in deliberate pursuit of the pop market, changed his style from a direct country sound to an unabashed commercial crooning. He even went so far as to appear on stage in a tuxedo, backed by a full string orchestra. He left the Opry in 1948 and went on to appear as guest personality on many top TV shows. Some diehard country fans began to desert him, accusing him of abandoning his country roots and joining the pop world.

Among Eddy's endless list of hits were *It's a Sin, Bouquet of Roses, Cattle Call, What's He Doing in My World?,*

Facing page: *Eddy Arnold, the Singing Plowboy, claims to have sold more than 70 million records during his long and influential career. Graduating in the 1930s from Pee Wee King's Golden West Cowboys, his smooth, crooning style brought him solo success.*

Below: *Red Foley was a regular performer on the Opry in the 1940s. Prior to that he had initiated the Renfro Valley show in 1939. Composer of the classic tear jerker,* Old Shep, *he turned increasingly later in his career to religious material.*

Make the World Go Away, and *Turn the World Around*. Whatever the arguments for or against Eddy's fidelity to country music, the people who know had no doubt whatsoever: they elected him to the Country Music Hall of Fame in 1966.

Red Foley

Clyde Julian 'Red' Foley, one of the all-time country greats, had a number of 'firsts' to his name. He was the first country star to have a radio network show; he hosted one of the first successful country TV series; and was one of the first singers to record more than a million sales with gospel music. Red Foley was born in Bluelick, Kentucky in 1910. After a distinguished few years in high school and college where he starred as a first class athlete, he moved to Chicago to join John Lair's Cumberland Ridge Runners – a 1930s string band that sparkled with individual talent and was a staple ingredient of the WLS National Barn Dance.

Some years later, Foley and Lair initiated the Renfro Valley Show. Then came the network radio show, Avalon Time, in which he co-starred with Red Skelton. During the 1940s he was a regular at the Grand Ole Opry, and in 1954 was invited to host the Ozark Jubilee Show from Springfield, Missouri, on ABC TV. Co-starring with Fess Parker, he appeared as an actor in the ABC TV series *Mr Smith Goes to Washington*, in the early 1960s. He continued touring extensively in the 1960s in between frequent radio and TV appearances.

The list of his hits look as if they might fill a small volume. They include *Candy Kisses, Tennessee Saturday Night, Chattanooga Shoe Shine Boy, Peace in the Valley* (which won a gold disc), *A Satisfied Mind,* and a host of others.

Foley was an outstanding pioneer of the modern country sound, but less publicized was the helping hand he gave to many an aspiring country star,

Left: *Jim Reeves, known as Gentleman Jim, had a velvety-voiced, soporific approach to a wide variety of material which greatly appealed to middle-of-the-road audiences. He entered the charts as long ago as 1953 with* Mexican Joe *(an eventual No 1), but 20 years after his death in a plane crash in 1964, fresh or re-recorded material was still being released and winning worldwide appreciation.*

Facing page: *Red Foley (seen here with would-be cowboy Tex Ritter) became head of The Ozark Jubilee Show in 1954, one of the first country style shows to be seen on TV. Among his many hits were* Tennessee Saturday Night, Candy Kisses, *and* Peace in the Valley *(for which he won a gold disc). He was elected to the Hall of Fame in 1967, and died in harness a year later while on tour with the Grand Ole Opry.*

Charley Pride being one of such beneficiaries. His talent and popularity were suitably recognized in 1967 when he was elected to the Country Music Hall of Fame. Red Foley died a year later of a heart attack while on tour with the Opry.

Jim's determination

Velvety-voiced Gentleman Jim Reeves could barely talk straight in his youth, never mind sing. But his long months of training under a teacher of phonetics paid off in the end, and his embarrassing stammer was transformed into vocalizing of svelte appeal. Jim Reeves was born in 1924 in Panola County, Texas, close to where Tex Ritter first saw the light of day. As the youngest of nine farm children, Jim dropped the chores as soon as he could and turned his face towards a career in baseball. A star pitcher at the University of Texas, he was soon spotted and signed up by scouts from the St Louis Cardinals. But a serious ankle injury put paid to any pretensions in that line.

Jim married Mary White in 1947 and, having majored in phonetics and pronunciation, not unnaturally cast around for a DJ's job. He found one with station KGRI, Henderson, Texas. He went on to become an announcer with station KWKH, Shreveport, Louisiana. One of the shows broadcast by that station was the famous weekly Louisiana Hayride. Jim was the announcer and occasionally was allowed to sing. One night the great but erratic Hank Williams failed to show up and Jim found himself filling in. The audience liked what they heard and so did Fabor Robinson, head of Abbot Records, who happened to be there that night. He signed him up on the spot and, as a result, Jim became a regular on the show.

Jim's first release, *Wagonload of Love,* died the death. The second disc, *I Could Cry,* didn't do much better, but its B side, a novelty number called

Mexican Joe, soared to the top of the country charts in 1953. Much to his amazement, Jim had arrived. In 1955, when *Bimbo* flew to similar heights, Jim joined RCA and became a regular on the Opry. During the next nine years, he recorded more than 50 hits for his new label, with phenomenal sales all over the world. And it didn't end there. After his death, his indefatigable widow continued to release new and old (sometimes refurbished) Reeves material well into the 1980s. Among Jim's hits were unforgettable numbers such as *Am I Losing You?*, *Welcome to My World*, *Adios Amigo*, *Yonder Comes a Sucker*, and the international smash hit, *He'll Have to Go*.

In 1964, piloting his own plane near Nashville, Jim Reeves crashed to his death, his pianist Dean Manuel dying with him. In 1967 he was posthumously elected to the Country Music Hall of Fame. It seems clear, listening to that slick, mellifluous voice today, that Jim Reeves eagerly shed most of his country trappings as and when he could and crossed over to the greener grass of the Nashville pop sound. But by any standards the music he gave the world brought the highest listening pleasure to millions.

Kitty Wells: mountain singer

Among the dozen or so superstars of country music who peaked during the 1940s and 1950s, Kitty Wells is a must. She has arguably done more for Women's Lib with her unexpressive hauntingly down-to-earth voice than many a more strident protester. Her achievements in a field once notoriously male chauvinistic are remarkable. Deservedly described as The Queen of Country Music, she became the first female artist to get to No 1 in

Left: *Kitty Wells, the Queen of Country Music, recorded some 57 hit singles in the period from 1952 to 1968.*

Facing page: *Kitty Wells faces a rapturous audience with daughter Ruby. Kitty is married to Johnny Wright, one half of the popular vocal duo of Johnny and Jack (Jack Anglin). It was Johnny who persuaded his wife to change her name from Muriel Deason to Kitty Wells.*

the country charts with her *It Wasn't God Who Made Honky Tonk Angels* (a pointed retort to Hank Thompson's earlier bitter-sweet *Wild Side of Life*). She has had more hits than any other female singer in the country record charts. And for 12 years continuously, from 1952 to 1964, she was voted No 1 Female Country Artist.

Kitty Wells (whose real name was Muriel Deason) was born and raised in Nashville, and learned to sing gospel music at an early age. In her teens she performed on local radio and at dances and other socials, singing to her own guitar accompaniment. In 1938 she married Johnny Wright, one half of a successful duo with Jack Anglin (Johnny and Jack), who broadcast and toured with their back-up band, the Tennessee Mountain Boys. Johnny's choice of professional name for his new bride was taken from an old Carter Family favorite, *I'm a-Gonna Marry Sweet Kitty Wells*.

Kitty became a featured singer with the band, in between raising a family of three sons. In 1947 they guested on the Opry before moving on to stardom with the Louisiana Hayride in Shreveport. In 1952 they became regular members of the Opry, and Kitty signed a lucrative contract with Decca. That year she recorded *It Wasn't God Who Made Honky Tonk Angels*, which shot her into individual stardom and hugged the No 1 country spot for 16 weeks. Since then she has appeared in the country charts more than 70 times either solo or as a duetist with partners such as Roy Acuff, Webb Pierce, Red Foley, and Roy Drusky. Her hit titles included *Making Believe, Jealousy, Unloved, Unwanted,* and *Forever Young*. Her pure mountain style, tight with repressed emotion, came like a fresh breeze straight from the Appalachians to many listeners who wearied a little of the Nashville sound.

Kitty Wells has received many honors in her lifetime, and one of the greatest was to be made a member of the Country Music Hall of Fame in 1976.

Honky Tonk in the Hall of Fame

Lefty (William Orville) Frizzell was an ex-pugilist (hence his nickname) from Corsicana, Texas, who made honky-tonk singing and its life style his own. A great admirer of Jimmie Rodgers, Lefty sang for his supper in local bars for some years and evolved a rich-sounding voice that drawled its way through the verses in a curiously laid-back way. His Columbia recording in 1950 of the self-penned *If You've Got the Money, I've Got the Time* hit the country charts with an almighty explosion. To show that it was no freak, he went on to record hit after hit with almost boring regularity. At one time he had four records listed simultaneously in *Billboard's* Top 10, a unique achievement.

Lefty joined the Opry in 1952, moved to California where he appeared on radio and TV for five years, then returned to Nashville. A sudden influx of unaccustomed wealth and fame served only to weaken his patchy resistance to the bottle, and he finally succumbed to a stroke in 1975 at the age of 47.

Lefty recorded what is probably the definitive version of *Long Black Veil*, and his other hits included *I Want to Be with You Always, Always Late, Saginaw, Michigan,* and *She's Gone, Gone, Gone*. One memorial to Lefty's often unrecognized talents lies in the deep influence he had on some of his successors, notably Merle Haggard and Johnny Rodriguez. The other was his election to the Country Music Hall of Fame in 1982.

Left: *The lovable comedienne Minnie Pearl, Queen of Country Comedy, was originally a dancer and actress in the 1930s. Her career with the Grand Ole Opry began in 1940 and she soon developed the comedy routine for which she is best known and which she has adhered to for some 45 years.*

Facing page: *Ex-pugilist Lefty Frizzell had a patchy career, slipping in and out of the charts in the 1950s and 1960s. But his influence on later honky tonk artists such as Merle Haggard was deep and lasting. The Long Black Veil was one of his greatest hits.*

Many sides of Marty Robbins

Marty Robbins's career was so long and popular that he properly belonged to the 1950s period of country giants, yet he carried on into the early 1980s, seemingly as strong and as much in demand as ever. Born in Glendale, Arizona, in 1925, Marty hankered to be a singing cowboy, like Gene Autry. Following a few years' service in the navy, he took a variety of odd jobs in order to eat and save pawning his guitar. After playing clubs and broadcasting in the Phoenix region, Marty eventually gained his own TV show. One of his guests was Little Jimmy Dickens who was so impressed with what he heard and saw that he recommended Marty to a high-up friend in Columbia Records. As a result, Marty gained an immediate contract, his first offering, *Love Me or Leave Me*, being released in 1952.

Marty's great forte was his rich and versatile voice. It could, seemingly, adapt itself to any medium and he could sing as well as or better than the specialists in that medium. Country music, gunfighter ballads, pop, rockabilly, Hawaiian chants, or gospel – they all came alike to Marty and were performed with consummate ease and expertise. In the early days he loved to yodel, and his high, intimate voice would break at the dramatic moment, earning him the nickname of 'Mr Teardrop'.

Marty joined the Opry in 1953 and then followed a string of hits: *I'll Go on Alone, I Couldn't Keep from Crying* were in the best teardrop tradition. *That's All Right*, with its Presley association, showed what Marty could do in the rock 'n' roll line. Some blues offerings followed in the mid-1950s, *Singin' the Blues* and *Knee Deep in the Blues*, which did his international reputation no harm at all. After a nod to rockabilly with *Mean Mama Blues* came the great gunfighter ballad, *El Paso*. His *Devil Woman*, backed by tasteful acoustic guitar work in calypso style, brought the pop fans crowding in. The vast majority of Marty Robbins's songs were self-penned – he wrote about 500 in all.

In addition to his musical career, Marty was wedded to racing driving. He was a talented if sometimes foolhardy driver, and survived a number of dangerous crashes. He had also invested shrewdly in oil projects, owned a ranch, and several music publishing companies. In 1970 he underwent and survived open heart surgery, receiving a rapturous welcome on his return to the stage. He was elected to the Country Music Hall of Fame in 1982, just two months before his death in December of that year.

Comics of Country

Country music of the 1940s and 1950s was not all serious, tragic, or sloppy. It also had its lighter side. True, the humor was often cornball, earthy, and less than funny. But a few gifted performers attained stellar status merely by accentuating the ridiculous.

One such was Minnie Pearl. Named Sarah Ophelia Colley, Minnie was born in Centerville, Tennessee. In the 1920s she graduated in drama and for a while taught stage technique and dancing. Gaining a local reputation for humor, she joined the Opry as a welcome comedienne in 1940 and has remained with them ever since. Minnie's humor is largely visual, so she has had only one record in the Top 10 – *Giddy Up, Go Answer* (1966). She appears on stage dressed as an old-time mountain wife, complete with broad-brimmed floral hat (with the price tag still hanging from it), antique summer frock, and button-up shoes. Her patter varies only slightly, from the 'Howdee!' greeting, to her confidential confession that she is out to 'ketch fellers'. Her gentle humor, never spiteful or blue, appeals widely to family audiences and has ensured her undiminished popularity after 45 years with the Opry.

Off stage she is Mrs Sarah Cannon, a cultured and highly respected Nashville citizen, the author of a best-selling cookbook and owner of a chain of restaurants. In 1965 she was voted Nashville's Woman of the Year, and 10 years later was elected to the Country Music Hall of Fame.

Facing page: *Marty Robbins learnt cowboy songs and listened to tales of the old West at his grandpa's knee, in Glendale, Arizona. After work on local radio stations, his singing and tremendous repertoire of cowboy songs gained him a contract with Columbia. Among his outstanding successes in later years were* Devil Woman *and* El Paso, *the latter winning a Grammy Award.*

97

Right and below: *Homer and Jethro came together as a straight duo in 1932 and broadcast regularly over station WNOX, Knoxville. The partnership lasted for 39 years, until Homer's death in 1971. They included an occasional parody of hit songs in their act and soon found that the parodies went down better than their straight material. As a result, they turned more and more to comedy. Among their hit parodies were* The Battle of Kookamonga, That Hound Dog in the Window, *and* Hernando's Hideaway. *They were both talented instrumentalists, Homer on guitar and Jethro on mandolin.*

Another veteran Opry regular is Grandpa Jones, essentially a vaudeville artist whose expert banjo picking (based on the style of Uncle Dave Macon) is interlaced with anecdotes, dancing, high kicking, and jokes. Louis Marshall Jones was born in Henderson County, Kentucky. In his youth he practiced assiduously on a cheap, just about unplayable guitar and became so adept that he took first prize of $50 in an Ohio talent contest in 1929.

Two years later he joined Bradley Kincaid's band on WLD, on the National Barn Dance radio show. It was from that show that Jones got the idea of appearing as an old grandpa, although he was only in his twenties. Audiences liked the idea, and with this encouragement he formed his own group, The Grandchildren. They became regulars on WWVA's Wheeling Jamboree and later on Cincinnati WLW. Army war service interrupted his career in the 1940s, but once that

was over he found himself a welcome Grand Ole Opry regular. He also became an established member of Hee-Haw, the enormously popular country music syndicated TV show that specializes in corny humor. Songs readily linked with Grandpa Jones's name are *Old Rattler, Mountain Dew,* and a couple of hits – *All American Boy,* and Jimmie Rodgers's *T for Texas.* Grandpa Jones was elected to the Country Hall of Fame in 1978, showing that humor sometimes pays.

Stringbean (David Akeman) combined the roles of virtuoso banjo-picker with that of comedian. The Kentucky Wonder, as he later came to be known, was born in 1915, in Annville, Kentucky. He must have inherited quite some talent from his banjoist father, because early in his teens he had built his own instrument, and in spite of being virtually illiterate, he very soon became an expert player. Stringbean joined the Lonesome Pine Fiddlers on WLAP, Lexington, Ken-

Bashful Brother Oswald (Beecher 'Pete' Kirby) was a master of the banjo and guitar, but it was with the dobro that he made his name. A star member of Roy Acuff's Smokey Mountain Boys. he resurfaced in 1971 to play his dobro with the Nitty Gritty Dirt Band on Will the Circle Be Unbroken.

tucky. He became an Opry regular during a three-year stint with Bill Monroe, and at various times also worked with Charlie Monroe, Red Foley, and Ernest Tubb.

Stringbean based his playing on the style of Uncle Dave Macon (who left him a banjo in his will). He is said to have earned his nickname from the aberration of an announcer who eyed the 6ft 2in performer and, forgetting his name, yelled 'Come out and play for us Stringbean!' The young banjoist cashed in on his willowy appearance, coming on stage in a shirt that reached his knees and belted pants that began just about there. In later years, after joining Hee-Haw he settled for a pork-pie hat, overalls, and horn-rimmed glasses.

In 1973 Stringbean and his wife had just reached their home on the way back from an Opry show when they were both tragically murdered by burglars on the premises.

A pair of doubles

Homer (Henry D Haynes) and Jethro (Kenneth C Burns) formed an extremely funny double act that lasted with interruptions from the 1930s through 1970. They specialized in taking the mickey out of popular country numbers, and were helped by some fine picking (Homer on guitar, Jethro on banjo). Initially they had their own radio series on WNOX, Knoxville, and later became regulars on the Renfro Valley Barn Dance. After an interruption for war service they came together again, appearing with great

Facing page: Stringbean (David Akeman), all 6ft 2in of him, was a well-loved comic entertainer and talented banjo player from Kentucky who had worked with Bill Monroe in the 1940s. Known as the Kentucky Wonder, he was highly popular among Opry audiences and especially on Hee-Haw. He and his wife were victims of an unsolved murder outside his home in Nashville in 1973.

success on various radio shows, guested on the Opry, and held a regular spot on Chicago's National Barn Dance for 10 years.

They recorded for RCA over a 20-year period and cut dozens of mockingly funny tracks, including *Baby Its Cold Outside* (with June Carter), *How Much Is That Hound Dog in the Window*, *The Battle of Kookamonga*, and *Hernando's Hideaway*.

The partnership ended after 39 years with the death of Homer in 1971.

Lonzo and Oscar were a long-running comedy team that kept audiences giggling (especially Opry folk) for years. The original Oscar was Rollin Sullivan, who came from Edmonton, Kentucky. The original Lonzo was Ken Marvin who sang with Rollin in pre-World War II days. A famous comedy song, *I'm My Own Grandpa*, was recorded by the original Lonzo and Oscar but was actually written by Rollin Sullivan and his elder brother John. When Marvin retired in 1945, John took his place as Lonzo.

It was this duo, the brothers Sullivan, who are chiefly remembered as Lonzo and Oscar, and who set the nation rocking with laughter. They toured extensively, appearing on various shows, with plenty of TV coverage. In 1947 they became regulars on the Grand Ole Opry.

John Sullivan died in Nashville in 1967. Rollin invited David Hooten to replace his deceased brother, and the act continued. There was less comedy in the new routine, with more emphasis on instrumental technique, aided by Hooten's superb mandolin playing. Memorable numbers by Lonzo and Oscar include *Take Them Cold Feet Out of My Back*, and *You Blacked My Blue Eyes Once Too Often*.

Right: *Tennessee Ernie Ford was originally a DJ in Atlanta and Knoxville. After he had moved to California, Cliffie Stone heard him sing and helped him land a contract with Capitol Records. Two early successes were* Mule Train *and* Shotgun Boogie, *the latter an early example of rockabilly boogie, which predated rock 'n' roll. But his greatest hit,* Sixteen Tons, *came later. Celebrated for his singing of religious songs, his* Hymns *became the first country album to sell more than one million copies.*

Facing page: *Lonzo and Oscar was the name of a comic double act that entertained Opry audiences for 20 years. The stage names hid the identities of the Sullivan Brothers, John (Lonzo) and Rollin (Oscar). The original Lonzo was Ken Marvin, who had teamed up with Rollin in pre-World War II days. After Marvin quit, Lonzo and Oscar toured with Eddy Arnold. Among their favorite songs were such masterpieces as* Cornbread, Lasses and Sassafras Tea *and* You Blacked My Blue Eyes Once Too Often.

Your "Mule-Train" Pal, Tennessee Ernie

6 Modern Mainstream

Facing page: Johnny Cash, the Man in Black, is arguably the best known country singer in the world. But success exacted its toll, and after years of hard work and exhausting tours, he became addicted to pills. His first wife could no longer cope, and divorced him in 1966. But his second wife, June Carter, had no wish to see him going the way of Hank Williams, and after a long struggle pulled him back from the brink of disaster to good health and a further string of hits.

There's nothing quite so hackneyed as the term 'living legend', but how else can you describe the charismatic figure of Johnny Cash? A member of the Country Music Hall of Fame (1980), who in 1969 swept up half a dozen CMA awards (best single, best album, entertainer of the year, best male vocalist, best vocal group, and outstanding service award), he is today probably the world's best known country singer.

John R Cash was born in Kingsland, Arkansas, in 1932. He boasts today of being one-eighth Cherokee on both sides of his family. His parents, Ray and Carrie, were impoverished cotton farmers, and besides Johnny there were eventually six other kids to feed and clothe. In 1935 the Depression drove the Cash family out of their home to a government resettlement project called Dyess Colony, in northeastern Arkansas. There, with 20 miserable acres to plow, and esconced in a dilapidated clapboard house sans electricity, they survived for 15 years. In 1937 the mighty Mississippi all but washed them out – an event recalled by Johnny in his 1959 hit, *Five Feet High and Rising.*

In 1950 Johnny enlisted in the Air Force, hoping to see action in Korea but was sent instead to Germany. To while away the time, he taught himself guitar and practiced songwriting. After four years' service, Johnny lost no time in marrying Vivian Liberto. The couple moved to Memphis, where Johnny met up with an outstanding electric guitar player called Luther Perkins, and bass player Marshall Grant. They decided to form a trio, calling themselves Johnny Cash and the Tennessee Two. After some amateur exposure on station KWEM, they gained an audition with Sam Phillips of Sun Records. Phillips eventually decided to wax two of Johnny's own compositions, *Hey Porter* and *Cry, Cry, Cry,* on one single. With early sales of 100,000, this single became a hit.

More records followed, all of them successful. They included *Folsom Prison Blues.* In 1956 Johnny joined Shreveport's Louisiana Hayride, and after the release of his million-selling *I Walk the Line* in that year, he found himself much in demand on tour. That last hit was the first of his records to make inroads into the pop market. There followed Opry membership, a stay in Hollywood for a B movie, and lucrative tours of Canada and Australia.

In 1960 the Tennessee Two expanded into the Tennessee Three, with the addition of drummer W S Holland to the group, and a year later Johnny began working with June Carter, daughter of the famous Maybelle Carter. It was during this period with Sun Records that Johnny claimed to have put together several unreleased tapes of gospel songs with Elvis

Presley — with, believe it or not, Elvis playing piano!

After more than a dozen hits on the Sun label, Johnny gravitated to Columbia in 1958, and with them he recorded a wealth of hits, including *Tennessee Flat-Top Box, I Got Stripes, Big River, Seasons of My Heart, Locomotive Man,* and *Don't Take Your Guns to Town.*

But the strain of touring – 300 days a year – was beginning to take its toll. In addition to hitting the bottle hard, Johnny was popping pills at the rate of 100 a day – some to keep him awake, others to calm him down. He was caught with 1,000 pills in his baggage on the US-Mexican border and was given a year's suspended jail sentence. He sometimes blacked out altogether; gigs were missed or fudged; and his weight went down so dramatically that the clothes hung on his 6ft 2in frame like a parody of Stringbean. To add to his misery his wife (who had borne him four daughters) sued for and eventually obtained a divorce. Gossip and widespread publicity that speculated on the parallels between Johnny Cash and the tragedy of Hank Williams did not help his cause.

Recovery and revival

It is a mark of the stature of the man that with the help of June Carter and Luther Perkins (who never deserted him), he pulled himself out of the depths onto a high plateau of complete health and wholeness, where he has since remained. To mark his return to better days, Johnny recorded an epoch-making single, *Ring of Fire,* in which he used brass in the backing for the first time. This chartbuster (pop and country) established a formula for similar follow-ups, including *The Matador* and *Understand Your Man.* Already accepted as almost one of them by the pop fans, Johnny set up a similar liaison with the folk world following his recording of *It Ain't Me Babe,* his friendship and association with Bob Dylan, and his singing with Dylan at the 1964 Newport Folk Festival.

It was in the mid-1960s that Johnny

began to record 'concept' albums, a unique idea among country artists. He built entire albums around a key subject, something very close to his heart. After this fashion he produced *Ride This Train* (1960), a hobo's eyeview of trains and railroads; *Bitter Tears* (1964), a plea for the underprivileged Indians; and *Ballads of the True West* (1965), which leant heavily on Johnny's considerable lore of those regions. To those were added *At Folsom Prison* (1968) and *At San Quentin* (1969), each of which sold more than a million copies and which were recorded live in their respective prisons before captive but enthusiastic audiences. After he 'got religion', Johnny did a religious album, *The Gospel Road,* recording the dialogue live in the Holy Land itself.

By now Johnny's entourage had swollen to include Mother Maybelle and the Carter daughters, Carl Perkins, and the Statler Brothers, among others. But in August 1968 they were struck a grievous blow when Luther Perkins was tragically burnt to death. He was later replaced by guitarist Bob Wooten.

The late 1960s were significant years for Johnny Cash. In 1968 he married June Carter, who has continued to give him her hundred percent support ever since. There was also a spate of successful singles to swell the family bank balance. They included *A Boy Named Sue,* which turned out to be his most successful single of all. Written by Shel Silverstein, it was played around the world to appreciative millions. Among other winners were *Orange Blossom Special, Daddy Sang Bass,* and *The One on Your Right Is on Your Left.*

Johnny recorded a couple of duets with his wife, June – *Jackson* (for which they won a Grammy Award), and *If I Were a Carpenter.* In the 1970s he went to Hollywood to star with Kirk Douglas in *A Gunfight.* There were also two more concept albums completed: *America: A 200 Year Salute in Story and Song,* which came out in 1972, thus beating the gun to the bicentennial by some four years; and

Facing page: Elvis Presley had his roots in country music in the two-roomed wooden shack in Tupelo where he was born. He was raised on spirituals and the music of Roy Acuff, Jimmie Rodgers, Ernest Tubb, and the blues singing of several black musicians. He also taught himself to play guitar. In 1953 he made an experimental recording for Sun Records. On one side was Arthur Crudup's That's Alright Mama *and on the other, Bill Monroe's* Blue Moon of Kentucky. *The first was a touch of rhythm and blues, the flip side pure rockabilly, and the single won acclaim when released in 1954.*

The Gospel Road, with dialogue recorded in the Holy Land.

Johnny Cash had throughout his life betrayed a leaning towards fundamentalist religion, but after his climb back to sanity and normality, his interest in things spiritual took a decided upturn. His concerts never failed to include a liberal sprinkling of gospel numbers and he developed a warm friendship with the evangelist Dr Billy Graham whose meetings Johnny often publicly supported. This was all in direct contrast to the ill-informed image of him sometimes spread by public and press. The media have portrayed him as a renegade, a tough, hard-living outlaw and ex-convict, forever being picked up by the police.

The truth is that Johnny Cash since his conversion is a model, law-abiding citizen, who enforces a strict no drinks, no smoking rule in his own recording studio. His two separate nights as a guest in a police cell were for minor violations. But it must be admitted that the image Johnny Cash projects on stage does tend to provide his critics with some of their smoke without fire. Dressed all in black, guitar brandished like a machine gun, Johnny sets his craggy, scarred face like flint as he launches into one of his dour convict ballads. But that uncompromising stance, coupled with his gravelly, off-key voice, is what makes it all strictly Cash.

Ernie Ford

One of country music's revered elder statesmen is Tennessee Ernie (Jennings) Ford. Born in Bristol, Tennessee, in 1919, Ernie eventually became so successful that during the 1950s his name was synonymous with country, and you could hardly pass a jukebox or a radio that wasn't filling the air with one of his hits.

He first worked as an announcer with local radio station WOAI. He moved from there to the Cincinnati Conservatory of Music, and in 1941 enlisted in the US Air Force as a bombardier. After the war he became an announcer on the country music station KXLA, Pasadena. There he joined Cliffie Stone's live Hometown Jamboree show, where his warm, intimate, bass voice prompted Stone to get him an audition with Capitol Records. Capitol gave him a contract in 1948, and from then on it was all systems go for Ernie.

His first releases, in 1949, were *Mule Train* and *Smokey Mountain Boogie*. These immediate hits were followed soon after by *Anticipation Blues, I'll Never Be Free, The Cry of the Wild Goose*, and a self-penned rockabilly effort, *Shotgun Boogie*, that topped the million mark. All this unalloyed success brought him a shower of engagements and his own networked radio and TV shows. But it was in 1955 that he hit the jackpot with his rock 'n' roll version of Merle Travis's famous coalmining ditty, *Sixteen Tons*. It stayed in the charts for six consecutive months and over the following decade sold more than four million copies.

In later years Ernie turned more and more to gospel numbers, and his best-selling album, *Hymns*, earned him a platinum disc at the end of 1973.

Brave girl from Kentucky

The typical rags-to-riches story in country music is epitomized by the life of Loretta Lynn, the coalminer's daughter who ended up one of the three most popular female country singers of all time and becoming in the process one of the richest women in America, earning more than the nation's President.

Loretta was born in Butcher's Hollow, Kentucky, the daughter of Melvin Webb, a grindingly poor coalminer. Married at 13 to Oliver 'Moonshine' (Mooney) Lynn, she was a mother for the first time at 14 and a grandmother at 28. The Lynns moved all the way to Custer, Washington, and there Loretta started in a small way singing professionally with a group optimistically named Loretta's Trail Blazers. She also started writing her own songs, largely based on real life situations. An obscure record company called Zero bravely opted to record the young lady, and their first release, *Honky Tonk Girl*, reached the Top Ten

Facing page, top: *Elvis Presley topped the country charts in 1955 with* Mystery Train *and* I Forgot to Remember to Forget. *The year before, he had appeared on the Grand Ole Opry and sung* That's Alright Mama *and* Blue Moon of Kentucky. *The audience was not impressed.*

Facing page, bottom: *Elvis Presley sings at the keyboard with his vocal harmony group, the Jordanaires. These began as a male barbershop quartet, but in 1950 sprang to fame with their participation in Red Foley's version of* Just a Closer Walk with Thee. *They joined Elvis in 1956.*

Chet Atkins is a man of many gifts, not the least being that of a master guitar player, for which perhaps he is best known. But he is also a talent scout (having discovered Dottie West, Charley Pride, and Roger Miller, among many others), and a prestigious record producer. The much publicized Nashville sound was initiated by his efforts.

in the charts in 1960. Neither the record company nor the Lynns could afford to plug the record in the usual commercial way, so Loretta and her husband motored to Nashville, trying to interest retailers and radio stations en route.

Their persistence paid off, and within months Loretta was appearing on the Grand Ole Opry. Early in 1962 she secured a lifetime contract with Decca, breaking into the charts again with the aptly named *Success*. From then on, she was practically never out of the Top 10, one of the greatest female hitmakers of all time. Her top solo efforts include *Woman of the World, Fist City*, and *Coal Miner's Daughter*. For some years in the early 1970s she partnered Conway Twitty in a series of best-selling duets that included *After Me the Fire Is Gone, Lead Me On*, and *The Letter*. She also partnered the same gentleman businesswise in the founding of a successful talent agency. Among Loretta's other widely varied accomplishments is the writing of her autobiography, *Coal Miner's Daughter* (nine weeks on the best-seller list), the award of CMA's Entertainer of the Year, 1972 (the first female performer ever to win the award), and the ownership of an entire town, Hurricane Mills, in Tennessee. Her autobiography became a film starring Cissy Spacek in the 1980s.

The Nashville sound of Chet Atkins

Superpicker Chet Atkins, whose guitarmanship earned him the 'Best Instrumentalist' award for 14 years on the trot, began his recording contract with RCA mainly as a vocalist.

Chester Burton Atkins was born and raised on a farm near Luttrell, Tennessee, in the 1920s. Despite his farming background, there was also music in the family. His father was no mean fiddler, and his elder half brother played guitar with Les Paul. Chet himself, an ardent Jimmie Rodgers fan, toured briefly with Bill Carlisle and Archie Campbell, after playing fiddle on WNOX, Knoxville. He tried to join Roy Acuff and His Smokey Mountain Boys, but failed

Facing page: *Hank Snow is one of the few Canadians to hit the American country charts consistently. After a rough upbringing spent on merchant ships as a cabin boy, he finally came ashore, taught himself to yodel and play guitar like Jimmie Rodgers, and in 1934 joined RCA. In spite of some Canadian hits, he had to wait until 1949 for his first American release. Since then he's been a regular on the Opry and has had scores of hits, including* I've Been Everywhere.

the audition. He achieved some consolation in 1946 by joining Red Foley on the Grand Ole Opry.

He settled in Nashville in 1950 as a busy session guitarist. Steve Sholes, in charge of country music for RCA, heard Chet's version of *Canned Heat* and was so impressed that he immediately offered him a contract. Chet's first solo album was *Gallopin' Guitar*, released in 1953. Within 10 years, Chet had climbed so far up the ladder that he had become an RCA vice-president. In his administrative capacity he helped to record a newly signed performer called Elvis Presley. The year was 1955, and the record, *Heartbreak Hotel*.

Perhaps more significant from a country point of view is that Chet Atkins is credited with being one of the pioneers of the 'Nashville sound'. That indefinable but very real music pattern is characterized by a relaxed, easy-beat, cool approach to instrumentation. To achieve this, country fiddles were tossed aside in favor sometimes of smooth violin sounds, guitars developed a rock beat, and the ripple of piano keys added sophistication.

Chet is a true virtuoso of the guitar, handling country, jazz, blues, flamenco, and classical styles with equal aplomb. His versatility and administrative successes brought him much deserved membership of the Country Music Hall of Fame in 1973.

Merle Travis

Country music has had more than its share of talented guitar pickers, and just a few of them could genuinely be called great. Possibly the greatest of these was Merle Travis. The fact that superpickers Chet Atkins and Doc Watson each named one of their offspring after Merle speaks volumes for his reputation. This multi-talented artist was also a singer, songwriter, actor, and cartoonist.

Merle was born in Rosewood, Kentucky, in 1917, and was taught guitar by Mose Rager, who learned his style from a black railroad worker called Arnold Schultz. Most of his long professional career was spent in California, where he specialized in Western and honky tonk songs. On his way up he played with various groups, including the Tennessee Tomcats, the Georgia Wildcats, Brown's Ferry Four, and the Drifting Pioneers.

During the war he served with the Marines, and later appeared in several minor movie roles. By then his services were much in demand among the major country bands of the period, including those of Tex Ritter, Cliffie Stone, and Jimmy Wakely. He also began to record some of his own songs on Capitol. *Divorce Me C.O.D.* and *So Round, So Firm, So Fully Packed* were both chart material, as was *Dark As a Dungeon*. But by far his greatest hit was *Sixteen Tons*, which was released in 1947 and made a heap of money for Tennessee Ernie Ford some eight years later. Interspersed with dozens of West Coast TV appearances was another movie, this time the award-winning *From Here to Eternity*, in which he appeared as a guitar-playing sailor.

Merle's songwriting, guitar-playing, and far-reaching influence on other instrumentalists earned him membership of the Country Music Hall of Fame in 1977, some seven years before his death.

Hank Snow

Another great singer/songwriter and guitarist, this time a naturalized US citizen originally from Liverpool, Nova Scotia, is Clarence Eugene 'Hank' Snow. A strict traditionalist who has no time for the modern commercial sound, he has always been a Jimmie Rodgers fan, even naming his preacher son Jimmie Rodgers Snow. After a desperately unhappy childhood, Hank served precariously on fishing boats in the stormy North Atlantic. In his spare time he taught himself guitar by listening to Jimmie Rodgers scratchy 78s. In 1934 he persuaded somebody at RCA-Victor to record two of his efforts: *Lonesome Blue Yodel* and *Prisoned Cowboy*.

Hank made little impact south of the Canadian border until 1949, when his recording of *Marriage Vows* hit the Top 10. A year later he became a regu-

Facing page: *Slim Whitman, a yodeling balladeer from Florida, had a modicum of success in the late 1940s but his first real hit did not appear until 1952, with* Indian Love Call. *There followed further hits in similar vein, such as* Rose Marie. *Slim's popularity in England is unabated.*

Below: *Hank Snow owes much of his success to the efforts of Ernest Tubb, who brought him to Nashville and had him guesting on the Opry. His top single,* I'm Movin' On, *was released in 1950 and remained No 1 in the charts for 26 weeks on end, staying in the Top Ten for more than 14 months.*

lar on the Grand Ole Opry, and his own great hit composition, *I'm Moving On*, entered the charts to stay there for an incredible 44 weeks. Hank has remained with RCA for a record-breaking 46 years largely, no doubt, as a result of the spate of hits (some of them million-sellers) that poured from his pen and voice in the 1950s and 1960s. Among them were *Rocket Rocket, I Don't Hurt Anymore*, and the tongue-twisting gazetteer recitation, *I've Been Everywhere*.

Over the decades, Hank has proved a popular ambassador for his type of music, appearing on stage in many parts of the world (including war zones) wearing his sequin-decked, snazzy cowboy outfits. A gentle man with a mellow voice and an expert touch on the guitar, Hank Snow earned his merited admittance to the Country Music Hall of Fame in 1979.

Transatlantic success: Slim Whitman

Slim Whitman is that strange phenomenon – an American country star who is more popular in Britain than he is in his own country. Born in Tampa, Florida, Slim, like Jim Reeves and others before him, was attracted more to baseball than music. By day he pitched for the Plant City Berries of the Orange Belt League and by night he did local gigs with his high tenor voice and guitar.

His 1949 recording contract with RCA resulted in the release of *Casting My Lasso to the Sky*, which attracted favorable comment but nothing much more. The same year he moved to Shreveport to appear on the Louisiana Hayride. Three years later he won a gold disc with his *Indian Love Call*,

Right and facing page: *Skeeter Davis, a member of the Grand Ole Opry for nearly a quarter of a century, began singing professionally while still at high school with her friend Betty Jack Davis. Known as the Davis Sisters, they scored a success with* I Forgot More Than You'll Ever Know, *which reached No 1 in the country charts in 1953 and was in the charts for 26 weeks. That same year they were both involved in a terrifying car crash that killed Betty Davis and left Skeeter seriously injured. After a long absence for recovery, Skeeter returned to take up a solo career. She won a gold record for* The End of the World, *in 1962, and then went on to appear at New York's Carnegie Hall. Her many hits have included duets with Bobby Bare, Porter Wagoner, and George Hamilton IV.*

straight out of operetta. His yodeling version of this hoary perennial, backed by wailing steel, set the pattern for many more hits of similar ilk. It was inevitably followed by *Rose Marie*, and as a result of this double success, Slim was invited to appear at the prestigious London Palladium in 1955, being the first country singer ever to star there. *Rose Marie* climbed to No 1 in the UK charts and sat there for 11 weeks, as attested by *The Guinness Book of Records*.

Slim's career seemed to nosedive through most of the 1960s, but in 1970 he played three concerts in the UK and was greeted with packed houses and a staggering reception. Record sales zoomed once more, winning him several gold discs. In 1974 he was back again in the UK charts after a long absence, with *Happy*

Anniversary.

Slim's musical sawish, featherbeddy voice breaks into falsetto at the drop of a chord and he chooses his songs accordingly. They tend to be swoony, romantic ballads picked from pop, folk, operetta, and light classics, although from time to time he nods towards his country roots with such offerings as *Cattle Call* (1955). Typical of his performances are *Danny Boy, When It's Springtime in the Rockies*, and *I'll Take You Home Again Kathleen*.

Success for Skeeter

Skeeter Davis, a protégée of Chet Atkins and a product of the Nashville sound, makes a better impression on disc than she does live. Her success has resulted in no small measure from grit, determination, and a devout faith. Born Mary Frances Pennick,

she was raised in Dry Ridge, Kentucky, one of seven children. Always attracted towards music as a profession, in her early twenties she teamed up with a friend, Betty Jack Davis, to form the Davis Sisters. Success seemed to be coming their way when their rendering of *I Forgot More Than You'll Ever Know* entered the Top 10 in 1953. Live gigs became plentiful, but that same year on the way to Cincinnati, their car was demolished by a speeding auto. Betty Jack was killed, and Skeeter badly injured.

After convalescence, Skeeter essayed a comeback by going on tour with Ernest Tubb, but the old magic was gone and showbiz saw no more of her until the late 1950s. Then Chet Atkins persuaded her to try recording once more. As a result she entered the charts with *Set Him Free* (1959)

and her own composition, *I'm Falling Too* (1960). She joined the Opry in 1959 and has remained a loyal member ever since.

But erstwhile fans began to have misgivings when her wide-ranging preferences brought her into partnership with such non-country greats as Duke Ellington and the Rolling Stones. *The End of the World*, released in 1963, won a gold disc and established her as an indisputable international star. There followed lucrative duets with Bobby Bare, George Hamilton IV, and Porter Wagoner. Among her solo items that became super sellers were *I'm Saving My Love, What Does It Take?*, and *Gonna Get Along without You Now*.

In spite of her acceptance by the pop fans, Skeeter advertised her predilection for country music with vigor. She is courageously outspoken on other topics, too. Her religious convictions have led her to refuse to perform in venues where liquor is served, and she has banned the growing of a profitable tobacco crop on her 200-acre farm. In 1973 she was suspended by the Grand Ole Opry for her strictures on the Nashville police during a WSM radio program. To an outsider, her comments might have seemed not unreasonable following hard on the heels of the murder of Stringbean and his wife (the murderer was never caught), and the razing by an arsonist of Tom T Hall's home.

Hitmakers from the Hayride
With a total of 68 hits to his credit, Webb Pierce must have set up some kind of a record. With his nasal twang and heavy electric backing, he epitomized a trend in Nashville that rose quickly to the top in the 1950s and 1960s, and just as precipitately tumbled right out of fashion thereafter. Born in West Monroe, Louisiana, in 1926, Webb came to prominence with the Louisiana Hayride in the early 1950s, and there rubbed shoulders with other nascent stars such as Floyd Cramer, Faron Young, and Jimmy Day.

After scoring some hits with Decca, which included his co-written *Last Waltz,* and *Wandering Back Street Affair,* he moved to Nashville and joined the Opry. His great barroom hit, *There Stands the Glass* (1952), was played endlessly on roadhouse jukeboxes throughout the land. Booze, shady joints, and jails were recurrent themes. He revived with some success Jimmie Rodgers' *In the Jailhouse Now,* recorded a sop for the rockabilly fans with *Teenage Boogie,* and trespassed on Everly Brothers territory with *Bye Bye Love*.

As demand for his type of material waned (except among collectors of his early recordings), Webb relaxed into semi-retirement by the edge of his guitar-shaped swimmingpool.

A postwar star who appealed especially to Irish-American audiences was Hank Locklin. Born in McLellan, Florida, of which township he eventually became mayor, Hank had a hard time during the Depression but never relinquished his ambition to become a 'real musician' one day. Sustained by a pleasing lyric tenor voice, he was usually a welcome guest on many radio stations in the South.

After army war service, Hank was invited to join the Louisiana Hayride. His first hit came in 1949 on the Four Star label with *The Same Sweet Girl,* but he had to wait another four years, when he came up with *Let Me Be the One,* before he enjoyed Opry recognition and was deemed good enough to transfer to the RCA label.

It was then that the Top 10ers began to flow. *Please Help Me, I'm Falling, Geisha Girl, Happy Journey,* and *It's a Little More Like Heaven* built up an army of fans for him. *Please Help Me, I'm Falling* (1960) was his own composition, went to No. 1 in the charts, and gained him a golden disc. Thinking that he was evidently on to a good thing, Hank recorded the same number again in 1970, this time with Danny Davis' Nashville Brass. It did not do as well second time round.

In 1957 Hank Locklin took part in the first country artists' tour of Europe, and by his many visits to Ireland has had much to do with the popularity of country music in that

Facing page, top: Skeeter Davis joins her old partner George Hamilton IV on stage in London to sing a few duets in remembrance of former days. Skeeter has long been a firm favorite in England, her hit End of the World *entering the British charts in 1963. George, in his impeccable suits, sometimes looks more English than the English.*

Facing page, bottom: Webb Pierce stands beside his fantastically customized car. In the 1950s he became the leader of the heavy electrified country rock then prevalent. Some of his rockabilly hits of that period are now collectors' items. Among his most memorable hits were Bye Bye Love, In the Jailhouse Now, *and* Tupelo County Jail.

119

part of the world. In his spare time Hank is an avid collector – among the items are early phonograph cylinders and racehorses.

The man who made people laugh

'Little' Jimmy Dickens, fully grown, stands just under 5ft, hence the affectionate soubriquet. Friends also call him 'Tater'. The youngest of 13 children, he was born in Bolt, West Virginia, in 1925. Raised on a ranch and educated at the University of West Virginia, Jimmy achieved some success broadcasting over local radio stations. But his big day came when Roy Acuff invited him to guest with the Grand Ole Opry. He did so well that he was quickly brought back as a regular.

Jimmy's specialities were lively, sometimes slightly outrageous novelty pieces, and his listeners loved them. He had to wait until 1949 for his first hit, *Take an Old Cold Tater and Wait*, on the Columbia label. Other successful offerings followed: *Pennies for Papa, A-Sleepin' at the Foot of the Bed*, and *The Violet and the Rose*. But it was his No 1 chart hit in 1965 that ensured his international fame. The title, *May the Bird of Happiness Fly Up Your Nose*, once heard, was never forgotten.

Little Jimmy Dickens insists that he was the first country artist to encircle the globe on a world tour. In later years he certainly toured most of the popular national TV shows, including dates with Hee-Haw and Johnny Carson. In 1983 he found himself a member of the Country Music Hall of Fame.

Faron Young

A durable and popular country entertainer who has lasted all the way from the early 1950s into the 1980s, is Faron Young. Hailing from Shreveport, Louisiana, his talented singing to his own guitar accompaniment carried him into the Louisiana Hayride. There he caught the eye and ear of Webb Pierce and became his protégé. Faron's style in those days was an embarrassing copy of Hank Williams, but he later developed an unmistakable crooning gloss to his voice that carried him acceptably into

the pop charts. After a spell in the army during the Korean War, Faron joined the Grand Ole Opry in 1953.

For more than two decades he appeared almost every week in the country hit charts. His rendering of *Hello, Walls* in 1957 reached the No 1 spot, and in 1971 his version of *Its Four in the Morning* sold close to a million copies in the US and half a million in the UK, remaining in the British charts for 20 weeks. Faron soon earned the title of King of the State Fair Circuit because of the phenomenal box-office sales that his presence guaranteed at state fairs throughout the land.

Apart from his stage appearances, Faron has been featured in a number of minor movies and has been seen on many TV shows.

Don Gibson

One of the greatest writers of country hits has been Don Gibson, and his two most famous songs, *I Can't Stop Loving You* and *Oh Lonesome Me*, were written in one afternoon. Don was born in Shelby, North Carolina, and first came to prominence on Knoxville's WNOX Tennessee Barn Dance. Wesley Rose signed him up as a writer on hearing one of his first compositions, *Sweet Dreams* (later recorded by Patsy Cline and Loretta Lynn). From then on a host of hits poured from his pen, but his performing career lagged behind. However, after recording *Oh Lonesome Me* with a Nashville sound backing, he was never again short of engagements. Among hundreds of popular favorites have been *Blue, Blue Day, Sea of Heartbreak, Give Myself a Party*, and *One Day at a Time*.

Ferlin Husky

Six times married and seven times a father, Ferlin Husky has been one of the most colorful characters to grace the country music scene. Born in Flat River, Missouri, he started out professionally as a disc jockey in Bakersfield, California, where his rich voice earned him a sizeable following. Convinced that his real name sounded too contrived, Ferlin adopted the pseudonym of Terry Preston, and it was under that name that he recorded

Facing page: *Little Jimmy Dickens is perhaps best known for his massive pop hit,* May the Bird of Paradise Fly Up your Nose *which rose to No 1 in the country charts in 1965. At 4ft 11in in his sox, he could hardly avoid the soubriquet 'Little', but his many successes over the years point to just the opposite in performance.*

Below: *Buck Owens managed to set up in Bakersfield, California, a rival country music recording center to Nashville. With his group, the Buckaroos, he developed a distinctive sound, based on a modernized version of the old western swing bands. With multi-tracked vocals he recorded many of his own hits, such as* Tiger by the Tail.

with Jean Shepard the duet *Dear John Letter,* which soared to No 1 in 1953. Ferlin also recorded some hayseed humor as Simon Crum, and in that guise his *Country Music Is Here to Stay* made the charts in 1958.

Terry Preston was eventually discarded as Ferlin recorded another great hit, his self-penned tribute to Hank Williams, *Hank's Song. Gone* sold a million copies, and subsequent hits included *Wings of a Dove, Every Step of the Way,* and *Sweet Misery.*

The hardy perennial: George Jones
George Jones, the Crown Prince of Country Music, has bounced in and out of the charts and on and off the Opry stage for more than 30 years. In spite of problems with women, drink, and drugs, which at times generated less than savory headlines, he still finds himself in the 1980s with hit after hit, at the very top of the tree.

Born in Saratoga, Texas, he recorded his first hit, *Why Baby Why,* in 1955 for Starday. During the next few years he flirted with rockabilly and came out with numbers such as *Rock It* and *Heartbreak Hotel,* under discreet aliases. There followed a long and fruitful period working with record producer H W 'Pappy' Daily, on various labels. Among more than 70 hits that were born from this partnership were *White Lightning, Tender Years,* and *She Still Thinks I Care.* George also recorded successful duets with a number of other artists, including Gene Pitney, Brenda Carter, and Margie Singleton. In 1963, with Melba Montgomery, he cut the chartbuster *We Must Have Been Out of Our Minds.*

In the 1970s George left Daily to team up with Billy Sherrill on the Epic label. The sounds at once became smoother and more pop-oriented, often with lush string backing. But that hard east Texas voice was still very much in evidence, and resulted in winners such as *The Grand Tour* and *The Door.* It was around this time, the mid-1970s, that George met and toured with and eventually married, Tammy Wynette. Their duets included *Near You* and *We're Gonna Hold On,* hardly prophetic in the light

of a subsequent divorce. At the beginning of the 1980s, George faced financial as well as marital and other personal problems. But such was his resilience that back he bounced once more with the million-seller, *He Stopped Loving Her Today,* and went on to win CMA Awards in 1980 and 1981.

She held her head up high
Regarded by experts as the most successful of all female country artists, Tammy Wynette (real name Wynette Pugh) well deserves her title of First Lady of Country Music, a title originally bestowed on Kitty Wells. Born in Tupelo, Mississippi, and raised on a farm, Tammy worked on a number of jobs, including a successful hairdressing stint, before she made her mark as a writer and singer of country songs. Married at 17, and divorced with three children to support by the age of 20, she needed the money. All in all, she went through five marriages, including a stormy seven years with country star George Jones.

After some preliminary success on Porter Wagoner's TV show, ace producer Billy Sherrill took her under his wing, and from then on things began to look up. In 1966 she had her first taste of success with a recording of the Johnny Paycheck song, *Apartment Number 9.* But it was her rendering of *Stand by Your Man* in 1968 that opened the floodgates. It won her a Grammy Award and became the biggest-selling single by a woman in the history of country music. From then on her story reads like a sensational novel. Her private life was full of pain and problems, including a terrifying kidnap attempt in 1978 from which she escaped quite badly injured. She experienced arson, burglaries and emotional upheavals. But her singing career blossomed. Hit followed hit, with numbers such as *Your Good Girl's Gonna Go Bad, D-I-V-O-R-C-E,* and *Kids Say the Darndest Things.* With ex-husband George Jones she also recorded some memorable duets, including *Southern California* and *We're Gonna Hold On.*

Tammy's sob-in-the-throat technique and the deep emotional treatment

Facing page: George Jones entered the country charts for the first time in 1955 with Why Baby Why. *Regarded by some as Hank Williams' spiritual heir, he has been called the Crown Prince of Country Music. Plagued throughout most of his career by drink and emotional problems, he married Tammy Wynette (with whom he recorded some notable duets) in 1969, only to be divorced six years later.*

of her songs, born doubtless out of painful personal experience, have earned her the award of CMA Vocalist of the Year in 1968, 1969, 1970, 1975, and 1976 and enabled her to sell nearly 19 million of her records.

Bill Anderson

A man who has been named as one of the top country songwriters of all time is Bill Anderson. In addition to the 1,000 or more songs that have flowed from his pen, he has also performed successfully for many years. Born in Columbia, South Carolina, Bill earned a bachelor's degree in journalism before turning to disc-jockeying for a living. His first big hit, *City Lights*, came in 1958. Among later compositions were *Riverboat, Po' Folks,* and *Saginaw Michigan*. Artists such as Ray Price, Jim Reeves, and Porter Wagoner were only too glad to get the chance of singing some of

these inspired lyrics.

Bill's own entry into the charts as a performer came with *That's What It's Like to Be Lonesome*, in 1959. He reached the No 1 spot three years later with *Mama Sang a Song*. His nickname of Whispering Bill was sometimes aimed at him in a derisory sense by detractors who claimed that he had no voice at all. He has also been accused of being too 'square'. But in later years he mellowed to the extent of abandoning his patriotic lectures and letting his hair grow longer. More recently he has devoted time and energy to acting on television and hosting chat shows.

Bobby Bare

That relaxed, folk-country singer and songwriter, Bobby Bare, came up the rags-to-riches way in anything but a relaxed environment. Born and brought up on a destitute farm in Iron-

ton, Ohio, he lost his mother when he was five, and because of extreme poverty, his sister had to be put out for adoption. Tragedy struck again many years later when his 15-year-old daughter Cari died of heart disease. Bobby sang, played, and wrote songs for nothing in between a series of menial jobs before drifting to California. Drafted into the army, he learned that an earlier composition, *All-American Boy* (under the pen-name of Bill Parsons), had made the charts. He received all of $50 for the copyright. Back in civilian life, things began to look up. Hit followed hit with titles such as *Shame on Me* (1962), *Miller's Cave* (1964), and *Four Strong Winds* (1964), which was first made famous by Ian and Sylvia. But his biggest success came with *Detroit City*, for which he won a Grammy Award in 1963. In the mid-1970s he put out a couple of

Facing page: *Bobby Bare, born on an Ohio farm, was one of the first Nashville 'outlaws'. Under the name of Billy Parsons, he recorded his first hit,* All American Boy, *in 1958. His biggest successes have been two country pop hits* Detroit City *and* Five Hundred Miles.

Above and below: *Truckers' songs, which first became popular in the 1960s, were supposed to have been inspired initially by Dave Dudley's classic,* Six Days on the Road. *The modern knights of the highway replaced the romantic image of the cowboys, and artists such as Kristofferson kept the giant wheels turning in song.*

Right: *Ex-marine and karate black belt, Freddie Hart finally fulfilled a lifetime's ambition in the early 1950s and became a country music recording artist, with the help of Lefty Frizzell. His first chart hit came in 1959 with* The Wall, *but he had to wait until 1971 for the big one,* Easy Loving. *With this he won the CMA Song of the Year award in both 1971 and 1972. Among the many hits that followed were* Bless Your Heart, My Hangup Is You, *and* Why Lovers Turn to Strangers.

Below: *Although Jerry Reed is one of the finest guitar pickers in Nashville, he first made his name as a songwriter with* Crazy Legs, *released in 1956. He soon evolved from being an extremely in-demand session guitarist in the 1960s to recording his own solo compositions with some success. His* Guitar Man *in 1967 inevitably went into the pop charts when Elvis snapped it up. His later guitar duets with Chet Atkins have become classics of their kind, and his comedy recitations, notably* Amos Moses *and* Lord, Mr Ford, *opened up new avenues for his talents.*

concept albums, *Bobby Bare sings Lullabies, Legends and Lies*, and *Bobby Bare and the Family Singin' in the Kitchen*.

Truckin' songs

Big Dave Dudley was born in Spencer, Wisconsin, a far cry from the acknowledged heartland of American country music. His ambitions, too, lay elsewhere. But his dreams of becoming a star baseball player bit the dust with a debilitating arm injury. After some years of trying his luck with voice and guitar on local radio stations in the 1950s, he suddenly found gold with an original composition, *Six Days on the Road* (1963). The song struck just the right note with the new breed of truckers, those kings of the highway who had taken over from the romantic cowboys and legendary but extinct railroad men. Soon the nation was ringing with that truculent, individualistic sound, and Dave was not slow to cash in on his success. There followed more titles in the same genre – *Truck-Drivin' Son-of-a-Gun* and *Trucker's Prayer*. Dave has a voice as big as his frame and his slightly slurred, mumbling style does more than justice to his theme. The truckers of Nashville presented him with a gold union card as a reward for putting their breed on the map.

Globe-trottin' George Hamilton

George Hamilton IV, 'the international ambassador of country music' may have dropped a notch or two in the US popularity stakes by reason of his tremendous following in most of the countries of the world. His bland, courteous, sober-suited looks, and easy, 'nice-guy' style appeal to Canadians and Europeans especially, and when he's in Britain he looks more like an Englishman than the Englishmen around him. Hailing originally from Winston-Salem in North Carolina, George enjoyed his first recording success with a John D Loudermilk pop song, *A Rose and a Baby Ruth*, in 1956 while still a freshman at the University of Carolina. It sold more than a million copies and was the first of a number of pop hits, including *Why Don't They Understand?*, *Only One*

Love, and *I Know Where I'm Going*. Around 1960, George decided to switch to folk and country music, moved to Nashville, and joined the Grand Ole Opry. Soon he was recording new hits such as *Before This Day Ends* and *Three Steps to the Phone*. In 1962 he recorded Loudermilk's *Abilene*. This reached No 1 in the charts and led to lucrative appearances in concert and on TV shows.

Songs of Loudermilk

One of George Hamilton's good friends and collaborators has been John D Loudermilk, a songwriter *par excellence*, from Durham, North Carolina. A born humorist, he jokes about the number of times the family had to move home in the early days – they were the original squatters, he claims. His homes almost equaled the number of jobs he held – or didn't – as he grew up, from janitor to Bible salesman. His musical training began as a drummer in a Salvation Army band. Today he performs his songs entirely solo with guitar and occasional mouth harp. Some time after leaving the University of North Carolina, where he met George Hamilton IV, he moved to Nashville. There, Chet Atkins took him under his wing and John never looked back. The hits that flowed from his pen have been recorded by most of the greats in country music at one time or another – Johnny Cash, Connie Francis, Chet Atkins, the Everly Brothers, and many more. He has written more than 500 songs, nearly 20 of which have topped the million mark. Favorites include *Tobacco Road*, *Grin and Bear It*, *Waterloo*, *Break My Mind*, and *Bad News*.

Above: *Singer/songwriter Don Gibson's crossover appeal has reaped for him rich rewards from his own performances and those of other artists. Born in Shelby, North Carolina, he early built up a following from his Tennessee Barn Dance broadcasts on Knoxville radio.*

Right: *Ex-Salvation Army bandsman John D Loudermilk, in addition to being a multi-instrumentalist, is also a composer of note. His* A Rose and Baby Ruth, *recorded by George Hamilton IV, eventually sold more than four million copies.*

Facing page, top: Porter Wagoner obtained his own syndicated TV series in 1960 and for seven years featured Norma Jean as his female vocalist. She left to get married, and Dolly Parton took her place. This lasted until 1974, when Dolly decided to go solo. Among the best of the albums with Dolly were Burning the Midnight Oil *and* Together Always.

Facing page, bottom: Loretta Lynn, the coal miner's daughter, was raised very poor and ended up being one of the richest ladies in America. Her first chart hit was Success, *in 1962. This was followed by a seemingly endless string of hits such as* Fist City, Here I Am Again, *and* Hey, Loretta. *There were also successful duets with Conway Twitty, including* Lead Me On *and* After Me the Fire Is Gone.

Below: June Carter, daughter of the legendary 'Mother' Maybelle, became one of a group known as Mother Maybelle and the Carter Sisters in 1943. In the 1960s they began to work with Johnny Cash, and June did much to help him back to health and sanity when he became addicted to drugs. Eventually they married, and recorded many hit duets.

Fighting Freddie Hart

Freddie Hart, from Kochapoka, Alabama, is bigger than life in more ways than one. One of 15 children born in grinding poverty, he ran away from home at age seven and worked at anything that allowed him to eat. At 14 he lied his way into the Marines and fought in some of the bloodiest campaigns of World War II. A black belt in karate, this gentle man also runs a school for orphans and handicapped children.

His musical career took off when Lefty Frizzell heard him sing, liked what he heard, and invited him to join his road show. His first big hit came with *The Wall*, in 1959, but this was eclipsed by his *Easy Loving*, which became the Song of the Year for 1971 and 1972 and stayed in the charts for 24 weeks. There followed another five consecutive No 1 hits, including *Bless Your Heart*, which became a memorable catch phrase. In the years that followed, few of his singles failed to reach the Top 5.

Buck Owens

One of Buck (Alvis Edgar) Owen's outstanding achievements was to turn his adopted town of Bakersfield, California, into one of the leading country music recording centers of the West Coast. So much was this the case that fans often refer to the town as Buckersfield or Nashville West. Born in Sherman, Texas, Buck and his sharecropping parents fled the Dust Bowl along with other refugees in the Depression years. They broke down in Mesa, Arizona, en route to California, and settled there. Buck tried his hand at most manual jobs in order to keep body in touch with soul. He married at 17, became a father at 18, and soon headed for the greener grass of California, where he settled in Bakersfield. By now an accomplished guitarist, he became a session man in demand, backing such luminaries as Sonny James, Wanda Jackson, Tommy Collins, Gene Vincent, and Tennessee Ernie Ford. He also played in honky tonk bars in Bakersfield and

eventually started vocalizing, much to the delight of the customers. This led to his writing his own material. Backed by his band, The Buckaroos, he introduced a strong element of percussion with more than a hint of rock into his performances.

Signed by Capitol Records in 1958, Buck came up with *Under Your Spell Again* (1959). There followed a string of hits, including *Above and Beyond, Under the Influence of Love, Act Naturally*, and *I've Got a Tiger by the Tail*. In the 1960s and 1970s, respectively, he recorded successful duets with Rose Maddox and Susan Raye. In 1971, against all the odds, he transformed the Paul Simon standard, *Bridge Over Troubled Water*, into a country hit.

The original US male

A man of rare talents, Jerry Reed (real name Jerry Hubbard), can claim distinction as guitarist, singer, songwriter, and movie star. Born in Atlanta, Georgia, Jerry spent teenage days laboring in cotton mills, and teenage nights in gin mills as an entertainer.

He obtained a contract with Capitol
Records in 1959 as a writer. Brenda
Lee liked his songs well enough to
record some of them, and in spite of a
two-year break for service in the navy,
his talent continued to blossom. His
explosive guitar picking earned him
rich rewards as a session man in Nashville, and in 1967 his *Guitar Man* for
RCA became his first hit and did
mighty things for Elvis Presley some
months later. Presley knew a good
song when he heard one and went on
to record Jerry's equally successful
US Male.

From then on there seemed to be no
holding the dynamic Mr Reed. Hit
followed hit in a career that buzzed
and scintillated. Among them were
Tupelo Mississippi Flash (1967), *Talk
About the Good Times* (1970), *Amos
Moses* (1970), which crossed over into
the pop Top 10 as well as making No 1
in the country charts, *When You're
Hot, You're Hot* (1971), and *Lord Mr
Ford* (1973). His two albums with
Chet Atkins, *Me and Chet* and *Me and
Jerry Reed* became models for aspiring
guitar pickers. He also found time to
appear in four movies with Burt
Reynolds.

A pure country sound
Porter Wagoner, the popular 'thin man
from West Plains', Missouri, has been
delighting country audiences for more
than 30 years. His shock of corn-
yellow hair and Nudie suits embla-
zoned with wagon wheels are a
guarantee of straight country music
with no concessions to rock, rockabilly or any other deviation. He trapped
and sold rabbits as a boy to pay for an
$8 guitar. Later, when a butcher's
assistant, he accompanied himself on
the instrument as he sang and advertised his shop's wares on the local
radio station. His popularity led to a
weekly appearance on KWTO,
Springfield, and there he was invited
on to Red Foley's Ozark Jubilee show.
His first recorded hit was *A Satisfied
Mind* (1955) on RCA, and others followed swiftly. *Eat, Drink, and Be Mer-
ry* was one of them, and so was the
gospel number *What Would You Do?*
Porter joined the Grand Ole Opry in

Facing page, top: *Charlie McCoy, wizard of the harmonica, hails from Virginia. In addition to making solo albums, he has always been in great demand as a session man, playing with scores of top artists, including Bob Dylan, Ringo Starr, Joan Baez, Perry Como, and Patti Page. Although the harmonica is his first and best love, Charlie is also an expert on trumpet, bass guitar, keyboard, and marimba.*

Facing page, bottom: *Eddy Arnold had the distinction of being the most successful country singer in America for 20 years, from the late 1940s to the late 1960s. During that period he claimed nearly 90 chart entries. His smooth, pop-oriented voice, heard in numbers such as* Make the World Go Away *and* Bouquet of Roses, *made him one of the first crossover artists and won him large new audiences.*

Above, left: *The Everly Brothers, Don and Phil, began performing together in 1945, by broadcasting on radio station KMA in Shenandoah, Iowa, when they were children. Their first great hit came in 1957, with* Bye Bye Love. *They followed this with more massive hits, which included* Wake Up Little Susie *and* Bird Dog. *In the 1970s they went their separate ways but were reunited in the 1980s.*

Left: *Merle Travis, besides being one of country music's great guitar pickers, was also a composer of note, a movie actor, an author, and a cartoonist. Among his compositions were hits such as* Dark As a Dungeon, *and the great Tennessee Ernie Ford success,* Sixteen Tons. *His innovative, complex, and sophisticated guitar style influenced countless other pickers, among whom was Chet Atkins.*

Facing page, top and bottom: *Tammy Wynette, best known perhaps for her recording of* Stand By Your Man, *won the CMA award for Best Female Vocalist of the Year for three years in succession (1968-70). That record also became the biggest selling single by a female artist in the history of country music. She adapted her plaintive style well to the heartbreaking themes of her songs, and was soon compiling more hits with numbers such as* D-I-V-O-R-C-E *and* 'Til I Can Make It On My Own. *She also wrote a frank account of her stormy marriage to, and divorce from, George Jones, in her autobiography,* Stand By Your Man.

Right and below: *Boxcar Willie, dressed as a hobo, brings a whiff of railroad nostalgia with him whenever and wherever he appears on stage. He relies mainly on traditional material in the Jimmie Rodgers and Hank Williams mold, punctuating his songs with amazingly lifelike locomotive whistles. His first successful single,* The Man I Used to Be, *was released in 1983.*

1957 and within three years was running his own syndicated TV series. His female star was originally Norma Jean, but when she retired for a trip to the altar, Dolly Parton took her place and remained there for seven years. His many duets with Dolly made recording history, and in 1969 their blended voices in *Just Someone I Used to Know* won them the Grammy Award. Among other duets were *Burning the Midnight Oil* and *Please Don't Stop Loving Me*. Porter on his own scored regularly with titles such as *Green Green Grass of Home, The Cold Hard Facts of Life, Cold Dark Waters*, and *Carroll County Incident*.

The unpredictable Roger Miller

By the 1960s, country music lyrics had by and large begun to grow somewhat stale and flat, if not unprofitable. It was time for a wind of change, and the man who breezed in to provide this was a zany jester called Roger Miller,

from Fort Worth, Texas. Raised in Erick, Oklahoma, on a cotton farm, he soon became a better-than-average guitarist, drummer, and fiddler. After service in Korea, he worked for a while with swing bands in Texas, and wrote and performed songs of his own. Almost broke, he wandered into Nashville, took a job as a bellhop, and spent the rest of the time trying to sell his songs. Eventually Ray Price recorded his *Invitation to the Blues*, and he was hired as a writer by Faron Young. Roger's *Billy Bayou* and *When Two Worlds Collide* were warbled into the charts by Jim Reeves.

After years of frustration, Roger found an outlet with RCA, performing his own songs. As a result, the hits began to pile up. *You Don't Want My Love* was followed by *Every Which-a-Way*, and *Swiss Maid*. But it was after he left RCA for Smash that Roger hit a purple patch with *Dang Me* (1964). This million-selling single earned him five Grammy Awards and became an international best-seller. It was quickly followed by *Chug-a-Lug, King of the Road, Do Wacka Do, You Can't Rollerskate in a Buffalo Herd, My Uncle Used to Love Me but She Died, England Swings*, and the plaintive *Little Green Apples*. Another six Grammy Awards came Roger's way in 1965 – a feat that has never been equaled.

His unpredictable but sophisticated nonsense broke all the conventions and earned him some abuse. But it tickled the ribs of millions way beyond country music, made Roger a rich man, and opened the way for new and equally unconventional talent in the shape of artists such as Kris Kristofferson and Tom T Hall.

Today and Tomorrow

Facing page: *Merle Haggard, born and raised in California, spent much of his early life quarreling with the law. This resulted in prolonged visits to reform schools and San Quentin. It is not surprising that his first recorded compositions, such as* The Bottle Let Me Down *and* Swingin' Doors, *were based on the seedy theme of prisons and barrooms. Later, with his group The Strangers, he recorded magnificent tribute albums to Jimmie Rodgers and Bob Wills.*

Country music in the 1980s presented a confusing kaleidoscope of sounds and styles. Even the boldest of crystal ball-gazers would have been hard put to it to predict a definite line of progression for the future. But one thing the experts were all agreed on – the music was growing phenomenally. This applied internationally as well as on home ground. The movies and television were not slow in coming forward to exploit the phenomenon, and introduced country artists into their programs sometimes on the flimsiest of excuses. The crossover tendency to pop, until the two became almost indistinguishable, was fiercely resisted by some of the diehard traditionalists, but it did bring in the money and a whole swarm of middle-of-the-road listeners who were not overly concerned about the music's label. So today there exist three broad streams which, if not actually confluent, flow in the same general direction: the traditionalists, such as Moe Bandy (with his honky tonk revivals), Boxcar Willie (in the tradition of Jimmie Rodgers), and Ricky Skaggs (with his bluegrass links); the outlaws such as Bobby Bare, Waylon Jennings, and Kris Kristofferson; and the crossover artists such as Roy Clark, Emmylou Harris, and Anne Murray, whose live appearances can guarantee 'house full' notices wherever they appear.

One thing was clear – whatever the future held, country music could face it confidently. It was alive, kicking, and growing fast.

Merle Haggard and The Strangers

The man who was eventually to topple Buck Owens as King of Bakersfield was Merle Haggard – a strange contradiction who was a traditionalist by inclination and an outlaw in life. The son of Okie immigrants to California, he was born in Bakersfield at the tail-end of the Depression years. Soon left fatherless, and with a mother who couldn't control him, Merle early became an arch-truant. Falling into bad company, he lived a teenage life of fraud, theft, burglary, and other differences with the law, finally ending up with a close to three-year stretch in San Quentin. Prison seems to have shaken him into his senses, and there he learnt to pick guitar, sing, and write a little.

On his release in 1960 he dug ditches by day, and played small bars and nightclubs by night. Soon he was discovered by Charles 'Fuzzy' Owens (who later became his manager) and made his chart debut in 1963 with *Sing a Sad Song*. In 1965 he reached the Top 10 with *All My Friends Are Gonna Be Strangers*, and from then on recorded with Capitol. Confident by now that he could write and record his own songs for a change, Merle began to turn out strongly autobiographical material. *I'm a Lonesome Fugitive* hit the No 1 spot in 1966, and this was followed by more in the same vein,

including *Branded Man* (1967) and *Mama Tried* (1968). But it was his *Okie from Muskogee* (1969), an ostensibly anti-hippie, a voice-of-the-silent-majority song (which earned him congratulations from President Nixon), that really caused a spluttering among his young fans. Merle had the grace to admit that it was a more-or-less tongue-in-cheek effort, and nobody was more surprised than he when it earned him a million dollars.

Merle cites his musical idols as Bob Wills (he owns his fiddle), Hank Williams, Jimmie Rodgers, and Lefty Frizzell. With his fine group of musicians, The Strangers, Merle has made serious contributions to country music history with memorial albums dedicated to Jimmie Rodgers and Bob Wills: *Same Train, a Different Time*, and *A Tribute to the Best Damn Fiddle Player in the World*, respectively.

Mel Tillis and the Statesiders
Mel Tillis, a favorite entertainer, claims to have written more than a thousand songs. Afflicted with a stutter, he turns the impediment to good use in his comedy patter, although it completely disappears in his singing. Born in Tampa, Florida, Mel hit Nashville in 1957 after a spell in the air force. His songs were soon in demand by artists such as Bobby Bare, Kenny Rogers, and Tom Jones. They included *Detroit City, Ruby, Don't Take Your Love to Town*, and *A Thousand Miles Ago*. From the 1970s onwards, Mel began to perform and record himself and scored with *Heart Over Mind, I Ain't Never* (originally co-written with Webb Pierce), and *I believe in You*. In 1976 he was voted CMA Entertainer of the Year, and with his musicianly backing group, The Statesiders, continued touring into the 1980s. More recently he has felt attracted to the movies and made a notable appearance in *Smokey and the Bandit II*.

Songs of the railroad
Boxcar Willie's sad train whistle sounds are so lonesomely realistic that listeners sometimes wonder if he hasn't got a genuine loco tucked away somewhere behind the drapes. Hailing from Sterret, Texas, Willie (whose real name is Lecil Travis Martin) first rocketed to fame in England during a 1979 concert tour. His father was a railroad man, and the family lived so close to the rails that the sound of trains was never absent. It was only natural that young Willie should be deeply influenced by the songs of Jimmie Rodgers and Hank Williams.

Willie did not feel the urge to become a professional country artist until around 1975. Before that he had tried his hand at many things – salesman, garage hand, shoveling manure, disc jockey, air force pilot. During his brief appearance in London in 1979 he appeared on stage in authentic hobo garb, punctuating *Wabash Cannonball* and other railroad epics with his eerie whistle – and the audience wouldn't let him go! Back home, he caused a sensation with a hit video and proceeded to record some of his 400 plus songs as singles. Among his LPs are *Boxcar Willie* and *Daddy Was a Railroad Man*.

Moe Bandy's breakthrough
Moe Bandy, Crown Prince of Honky Tonk, was born in Meridian, Mississippi, forever associated with Jimmie Rodgers. Moe's grandpa had worked on the railroads with the legendary father of country music and owned and played a collection of his records. So it was that Moe was just about weaned on Rodgers music. After moving to San Antonio, Texas, Moe earned a painful living bronco busting on the rodeo circuit, until a surfeit of broken bones persuaded him to quit. He took a day job as a sheet-metal worker and sang country music by night. By 1972 he had made a sufficient impression to be recorded, and a year later reached the Top 5 with his *I Just Started Hatin' Cheatin' Songs Today*. There followed *Honky Tonk Amnesia, It Was Always So Easy to Find an Unhappy Woman*, and other ditties with similar themes. But Moe really came into his own when he changed to the CBS label with producer Ray Baker and initiated a string of hits with blockbuster *Hank Williams, You Wrote My Life*, in 1975.

Facing page: *Waylon Jennings was one of Nashville's rebels, or outlaws. The latter name was used on a compilation album* Wanted: The Outlaws, *put out by RCA in 1976. Featured on it, with Willie Nelson and others was Waylon Jennings. The record was a success, selling more than a million copies, and it helped to bring Waylon to a peak that had been building up for some years before. He'd begun as a DJ in his home state of Texas, but formed his own group, the Waylors, after moving to Phoenix, Arizona, in the 1960s. Among his early chart entries were* Walk On Out of My Mind *and* Only Daddy That'll Walk the Line, *both released in 1968. In the 1970s, Waylon began to produce and record material in the way he wanted it, regardless of opposition from the Nashville hierarchy. He took new ideas from young innovative writers such as Kris Kristofferson and Billy Joe Shaver, which resulted in no-compromise numbers to whet the appetite of a record-buying public.*

Right and facing page: Willie Nelson, father of the outlaw movement and close friend of Waylon Jennings, was born in Abbot, Texas. After working in some of the hairiest honky tonk bars in Texas, and a spell in the air force in Korea, he started writing his own songs. There came a move to Nashville in the early 1960s, where his songs such as Crazy *and* Hello Walls *made an impact. But it took him many more years before he was accepted as a performer, in spite of his longhaired, denim-wearing image. He finally settled in Austin, Texas, and while there recorded a concept album for Columbia,* Red Headed Stranger, *which was a runaway success. It included a million-selling single,* Blue Eyes Crying in the Rain, *a crossover offering that firmly established Willie among the top country stars. In the 1970s he generated an explosion in country music popularity by rejecting the smooth Nashville sound in favor of a fusion of modern and traditional values served up in a spare, no-nonsense package.*

Bar-rooms and booze, cheating and heartbreak seem to be Moe's stock-in-trade. But he claims to be solidly country, hewing close to his traditional roots. Tens of thousands of enthusiastic fans, a large proportion of them in Europe, would gladly testify to that.

Outlaws

In 1976 a million-seller called *Wanted: The Outlaws* was released by RCA. It was a compilation album that featured songs by Waylon Jennings, Willie Nelson, Tompall Glazer, and Jessi Colter. These self-styled outlaws had gotten tired of Nashville's conformism but were also adamantly opposed to the crossover movement into pop. They preferred to do their own thing in their own way – 'sing and be damned' could have been their motto. This first defiant gesture resulted in mountainous sales and the keen interest of a large section of the rock and pop market.

Waylon Jennings was born in Littlefield, Texas. He became a local deejay at the age of 12, and a few years later was invited by Buddy Holly to become his electric bass player. He signed for RCA after Chet Atkins heard him with his group, The Waylors. After moving to Nashville, the rebel in Waylon brought him into a period of abrasive confrontation with RCA over what Waylon decided was a lack of artistic freedom. He made such uncompromising demands at RCA's head office in New York that he was able to break free from Nashville control and launch out with his own independent production deal.

Recordings that Waylon presented to RCA for release included *Ladies Love Outlaws* and *Honky Tonk Heroes*. Three years later came the historic *Wanted: The Outlaws*, and it was this album that not only pushed Waylon straight into the financial limelight but also did as much for his friend Willie Nelson, who was also intent upon bucking the system. They teamed up in several best-selling duets, including *Good Hearted Woman* and in an album titled *Waylon and Willie*. After a nod to his roots in 1975 with a hit single, *Are* *You Sure Hank Done It This Way* and *Bob Wills Is Still the King*, Waylon strode into the 1980s with *Good Ol' Boys* and the theme music for the TV series *Dukes of Hazzard*.

The father figure of the so-called outlaw movement was undoubtedly Willie Nelson. His career has paralleled that of Waylon Jennings in many ways – long years of struggle and conformism in Nashville in an attempt to get his songs accepted, followed by a sudden breakaway and change of image. Drugs, long hair, T-shirts, three wives and a succession of wrecked cars have all contributed to the hippie image.

Born in Abbot, Texas, Willie began his professional career in radio in the 1950s, both as deejay and performing musician. He had some early encouragement from *Family Bible, Hello Walls*, boosted by Faron Young, and *Night Life*, made famous by Ray Price. But his own jazz-influenced, discordant style of singing was so different from the Nashville norm that his personal efforts were largely

ignored. When his Nashville home was burned to the ground, this was the last straw. He fled back to Texas and settled in Austin. There he became a kind of father figure for a new hippie movement around whom younger musicians and fans alike rallied with enthusiasm. He inaugurated an annual festival at Dripping Springs in Texas, which he hoped would bring together the hippie element and the 'rednecks'. Music on offer was an amalgam of gospel, rock, and avant-garde country.

In 1975 Willie had a million-selling single, *Blue Eyes Crying in the Rain*, which was one of the tracks from his best-selling album *Red-Headed Stranger*. Three years later he recorded a number of pop standards in an album called *Stardust*, which is alleged to have sold more than three million copies. He won the CMA Entertainer of the Year award in 1979 and began a successful diversion as a movie actor. *Poncho and Lefty*, a well-received album of duets with Merle Haggard, was released in 1983.

139

Another member of the rebels who starred on *Wanted: The Outlaws*, was Jessi Colter, Waylon Jennings's wife. Born Miriam Johnson, in Phoenix, Arizona, Jessi is distantly related to one Jesse Colter, a member of Jesse James's outlaw gang who handled the counterfeiting – hence her stage name. Married to guitarist Duane Eddy in 1961, she confined herself mainly to songwriting at first. When her marriage broke up, she married Waylon Jennings. In *Suspicious Minds* (1970) she dueted successfully with Waylon, a single that did even better on its re-release six years later because it reached the No 2 spot. In 1975 she went solo for Capitol and her first LP, *I'm Jessi Colter* included a song that she claims she dashed off in five minutes. It was *I'm Not Lisa* and quickly sold a million copies as a single. Two more hit singles in the mid-1970s were *Whatever Happened to Blue Eyes* and *It's Morning*.

The most dashing outlaw

A contemporary outlaw who seems to have been everywhere and done everything is Kris Kristofferson. Superstar singer/songwriter, poet, musician, actor, helicopter pilot, athlete, boxer, Rhodes Scholar – you name it – Kris has changed the face of Nashville and has an enormous cult following among the younger set. Born in Brownsville, Texas, the son of a retired Air Force major general, Kris moved with his family to San Mateo, California. At school he excelled in boxing (Golden Gloves) and writing. He edited a sports paper and won short story writing contests in *Atlantic Monthly*. In 1958 he won a Rhodes Scholarship to Oxford, England. There he achieved a Master's degree in English, returned to the States, married and joined the Army as a helicopter pilot. But all the time the poet in him kept him relentlessly writing songs.

Before taking up a teaching job at West Point, Kris visited Nashville for a brief stay. Introduced to Johnny Cash, and liking what he saw and heard there, he resigned from the Army, left his wife, and opted for a singer and songwriter as his future profession. He moved to Nashville in 1965. To begin with, it meant getting down to the nitty gritty. In order to survive, he took cleaning jobs, served as a janitor, and did some more helicopter flying.

His big break came when Roger Miller took a fancy to three of his songs and recorded them. They were *Me and Bobby McGee*, *Casey's Last Ride*, and *Barby's Castle*. From then on, Kris's songs were much in demand. *For the Good Times* appealed to both Ray Price and Bobby Bare; Roy Drusky sang *Jody and the Kid*; and both Johnny Cash and Ray Stevens brought out their versions of *Sunday Morning Coming Down*.

Kris's own recording career dates from 1970, when he launched the album *Kristofferson*; on re-issue the title was changed to *Me and Bobby McGee*. In 1973 the single *Why Me* topped the charts. He was married again, this time to Rita Coolidge, with whom he recorded several best-selling duets, although the marriage was not to last. In the late 1970s and early 1980s Kris became a star attraction in Hollywood. He appeared in *Pat Garratt and Billy the Kid*, *Alice Doesn't Live Here Anymore*, *A Star Is Born*, *Vigilante Force*, and several more movies.

Always a man who believes in doing his own thing, Kris has revolutionized songwriting in Nashville with a poet's contemporary awareness of the wider horizons of country music. As a result, his memorable songs appeal to ever wider audiences.

Glenn Campbell, perfectionist

Artists who started out singing, playing, and writing pure country and later crossed over to appeal to the much larger pop-fed public proliferated in the 1970s and 1980s. A leader in this group is ex-session man Glen Campbell. Glen, the seventh son of a seventh son in a 12-child family, was born in the euphemistically named community of Delight, Arkansas. His musical parents taught him guitar very early in life – a skill that he developed profitably in the years ahead.

Facing page: *Jessi Colter (who took her name from a distantly related ancestor, the counterfeiter Jesse Colter), was already a church pianist at age 11. After marrying and touring with rock 'n' roll guitarist Duane Eddy for eight years, she married Waylon Jennings, and happily joined his outlaw band. Her songwriting talents have been recognized and recorded by artists such as Dottie West, Anita Carter, and Don Gibson, and her own recording of* I'm Not Lisa *was a huge crossover hit.*

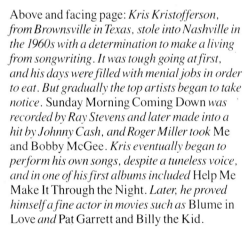

Above and facing page: *Kris Kristofferson, from Brownsville in Texas, stole into Nashville in the 1960s with a determination to make a living from songwriting. It was tough going at first, and his days were filled with menial jobs in order to eat. But gradually the top artists began to take notice.* Sunday Morning Coming Down *was recorded by Ray Stevens and later made into a hit by Johnny Cash, and Roger Miller took* Me and Bobby McGee. *Kris eventually began to perform his own songs, despite a tuneless voice, and in one of his first albums included* Help Me Make It Through the Night. *Later, he proved himself a fine actor in movies such as* Blume in Love *and* Pat Garrett and Billy the Kid.

For about five years Glen was a member of his uncle's band, playing mainly in Albuquerque, New Mexico. He left to form his own band, but hunger eventually drove him to session work. His instrumental expertise soon brought him plenty of work, recording with Frank Sinatra, Presley, Nat King Cole, Dean Martin, and a host of other celebrities. He also gained valuable experience playing guitar in a variety of styles from classical to rock.

In 1967 Glen finally made it in the big time. His recording of John Hartford's *Gentle on My Mind* was a smash hit in both country and pop charts. There followed his version of Jim Webb's *By the Time I Get to Phoenix*, which won a hatful of awards. Webb, soon to become a close friend, provided Glen with two more pop-country blockbusters, *Wichita Lineman* and *Galveston*. From then on, hit followed hit, both solo and in duets with Bobbie Gentry and later Anne Murray.

In 1975 he had a massive success with *Rhinestone Cowboy*, followed by *Southern Nights* two years later. Glen had no illusions about his music. He claimed that there were only two kinds of music – 'good and bad', and he made sure his was always good by using strings, choruses, full symphony orchestras, and anything that might enhance his backing sounds. This quest for perfection, allied to his all-American boyish good looks, also helped his excursions into the movie business. He played a convincing role in Paramount's *True Grit*, with John Wayne, but did less well in a second film, *Norwood*.

Dolly's hard road to fame

International superstar Dolly Parton, the buxom blonde from Locust Ridge in the mountains of Tennessee, came up the hard way like so many of her contemporaries. But a burning ambition, innate musicianship, a shrewd business sense, and a figure that was more than easy on the eye all helped to

Right: *Dolly Parton, one of 12 children, grew up in a family so poor that they had to pay the doctor who delivered her with a sack of cornmeal, so the story goes. At 10 she was already appearing on Knoxville radio and TV, and at 13 had cut her first record and taken her first bow on the stage of the Grand Ole Opry. In 1967 she joined Porter Wagoner's show and with him scored a duet success performing Tom Paxton's* Last Thing On My Mind. *Her first No 1 came in 1970 with* Joshua.

Facing page: *Glen Campbell, with his cleancut appearance, looked the ideal All-American Boy. But he had other things going for him too. For one, he became a talented musician, mastering particularly the six- and twelve-string guitars. In Los Angeles he worked as a session man for Capitol Records and played for a diverse procession of artists, including Frank Sinatra, Elvis Presley, Jack Jones, and Nat King Cole. His 1967 crossover hit,* By the Time I Get to Phoenix, *won him a string of awards.*

place her on her present pedestal. The family of a dozen children were raised 'dirt poor', but with love.

Dolly was composing before she could read or write, and sang continually through all her chores. At age 10, she appeared on Cas Walker's TV shows, and in 1959, aged 13, she made her first record, *Puppy Love*. In 1964 she left high school and headed straight for Nashville, boarding at first with an uncle. In 1967 Porter Wagoner invited her to join his road show to replace Norma Jean. Dolly stayed with Porter for six or seven years. Their duets, which kicked off with Tom Paxton's *The Last Thing on My Mind* (a Top 10 hit), caught the public fancy and Dolly's reputation burgeoned.

Signed up by RCA, Dolly's songwriting talents blossomed into offerings such as *Joshua* (1970), *Coat of Many Colors* (1971), *My Tennessee Mountain Home* (1973), *Jolene* (1973), *Love Is Like a Butterfly* (1974), and

The Bargain Store (1975), all enormous hits and aimed at the widest possible audience.

In 1974 Dolly left Porter to form her own band, made up mainly from members of her own family. Moving to Los Angeles two years later, she edged further towards the pop market with songs such as *Have You Come Again* and *Two Doors Down*. In 1978 she won the CMA Entertainer of the Year award, and hard on the heels of numerous TV shows, broke into movies in the 1980s in a film called *9 to 5*.

Kenny Rogers

Multi-millionaire Kenny Rogers, one of the highest paid entertainers in the world, was near bankruptcy shortly before his recording of *Lucille* started his meteoric rise to superstardom. Born in Houston, Texas, one of a family of eight children, he sang in the church choir, played bass, piano, and guitar, and with some schoolmates formed a group called The Scholars.

Their recording of *Crazy Feeling* scored a minor success on a Houston label. His professional experience began with a jazz group, The Bobby Doyle Trio, with whom he toured for some years. In 1966 he turned folksy and joined The New Christy Minstrels. Together with three others of The Minstrels he eventually broke away to form The First Edition. A number of hits ensued, including *Just Dropped In to See What Condition My Condition's In*, *Ruby Don't Take Your Love to Town*, *Somethin's Burnin'*, and *Reuben James*.

In 1975, Kenny signed with United Artists, and with producer Larry Butler behind him started out promisingly with *Love Lifted Me*, *Homemade Love*, and *Laura*. But it was *Lucille*, in 1977, that raised him to the No 1 spot in country and pop charts and sold millions of copies in the States and abroad. Then came *Daytime Friends*, another million-seller. More country songs followed – *The Gambler* in 1978

145

and *Coward of the County* a year later. Towards the end of the 1970s Kenny's voice, gritty and grainy at best, found its ideal foil in that of Dottie West. Together they hosted a number of TV shows and repeatedly hit the charts as duetists with songs such as *All I Ever Needed Is You* and *'Til I Can Make It on My Own*. In 1983 Kenny switched to RCA, his first single being a million-selling effort with Dolly Parton, *Islands in the Sun*.

With all these successes, Kenny has been swamped with awards of all kinds. Along the way he also managed to build up a Fort Knoxlike bank balance. A recent tour with Dolly Parton earned him 200,000 dollars a night, and two of his palatial homes are valued at 14 million dollars, not including his 86 Arabian horses worth 6 million dollars. There is also a private jet, a helicopter, Rolls-Royces, a Jaguar, a Ferrari, and a 600,000-dollar yacht ... all glittering testimony to the earning power of a superstar.

Emmylou Harris

A female artist of tremendous talent and appeal who, in the mid-1980s was striding forward across the top of the country, rock, and pop charts is Emmylou Harris. Born in Birmingham, Alabama, Emmylou at first tried her luck in the folk clubs of Washington and New York, with no success at all. But at one club the Flying Burritos heard her, liked her voice, and invited her to join them. However, before she could do so, the outfit fell apart. Gram Parsons, the great country rock exponent, was a member of the band at that time, and when he left he took Emmylou with him to Los Angeles. There she participated in Parson's celebrated LPs, *GP* and *Grievous Angel*.

Emmylou's tour with Parsons was ended in 1973 by his tragic and untimely death. Emmylou returned to Washington and formed her own group, Angelband. In the meantime Warner's had been listening to her singing on Parson's last album and promptly acquired her for their Reprise label. Her first album, released in 1975, was *Pieces of the Sky*. It con-

tained just about everything – Merle Haggard's *The Bottle Let Me Down*, Dolly Parton's *Coat of Many Colors*, the Louvin Brothers' *If I Could Only Win Your Love* (which also hit No 1 in the country charts as a single), and songs by The Beatles, Waylon Jennings, and The Everly Brothers. Performed with a country rock approach, it soared to success both in America and Britain.

By now Emmylou had shrewdly chosen her backing group. Known as The Hot Band, most of them had worked with Parsons and included some of the most expensive and talented musicians ever to appear on the rock circuit. They did much to establish her firmly in the country rock scene.

In 1976 there appeared a second LP, *Elite Hotel*, which successfully repeated the previous formula. A year later came *Luxury Liner*, in which her famous Hot Band was prominently featured. In 1983, although by then the darling of rock, pop, and country fans, she defied the crossover trend by moving back to Nashville from Los Angeles, thus symbolically underlining her traditional country leaning.

A touch of refinement

The Gentle Giant of Country Music, Don Williams, is a lean, stetson-toting man of few words and gentle persuasions. Born in Plainview, Texas, Don helped to form the Pozo Seco Singers, a folk/pop trio in the 1960s. They had their successes, such as *I Can Make It with You*, *Time*, and *Louisiana Man*, but they disbanded in 1971 because of the decline in the folk boom.

Don returned to Texas to work in the furniture trade, but a year later he was invited to Nashville to write songs for a music publishing company. From there it was only a step to recording his own material on the obscure JMI label. As a result, Don recorded *Don't You Believe?* and *The Shelter of Your Eyes*, the latter becoming a country chart entrant. There followed in 1973 the *Don Williams Vol 1* album, in 1978 *Images*, which won him the CMA Vocalist of the Year award, and in 1979 *New Horizons*. In England, his

Facing page, top: *Emmylou Harris began as an unsuccessful folk singer, but eventually found success with country music, after a good deal of encouragement from Gram Parsons. A major element in her triumph has been the backing of her Hot Band, a group of superlative musicians who are almost as famous as Emmylou herself. In 1979 she won the CMA Female Vocalist award with her country-flavored* Blue Kentucky Girl.

Facing page, bottom: *Don Williams, the balladeer with the confidential, laid-back style, appeals almost equally to country and pop fans. Before taking up a solo career, he had formed a group called the Pozo Seco Singers, who sang a mixture of folk, pop, and country. In 1975 he notched up his first No 1 with* You're My Best Friend. *Three years later, his* I Recall a Gypsy Woman *outsold every other kind of popular music record in Britain, and contributed to his being voted Country Artist of the Decade in a 1980 English poll.*

unruffled, underplayed but precise performances, tinged with evident sincerity, gained him a host of friends and several gold discs. Don has also made a movie with Burt Reynolds and Jerry Reed, *WW and the Dixie Dance Kings*.

Black breakthrough

The first black country singer to achieve any kind of success was probably DeFord Bailey, in the late 1920s, and there have been a few minor male black artists since then. But the first black superstar was without question Dallas-based millionaire Charley Pride. Born in Sledge, Mississippi, one of 11 children, Charley spent his childhood picking cotton, listening to Acuff, Williams, and Tubb on an old battery radio, and singing country songs to his own guitar accompaniment. His great ambition was to become a baseball star – an ambition almost achieved when he played in the Negro American League with Detroit and the Memphis Red Sox. After two years in the Army, he returned to marry and move to Montana where he worked as a zinc smelter by day and a nightclub entertainer by night.

One evening he was heard by Red Sovine, who was so impressed with his voice that he recommended a trip to Nashville. After a recording session there, Chet Atkins signed him to an RCA contract. The color of Charley's skin caused some flutters in the RCA dovecote because the executive were unsure about white reaction in the South. They need not have worried. Charley's magnificent voice and expert styling broke through all barriers and well and truly integrated country music from that day on. His first effort was *The Snakes Crawl at Night* (1966), and within a few months he had entered the charts with *Just Between You and Me*. He made his debut on the Grand Ole Opry in 1967 and still occasionally appears there. His list of awards, national and international, would fill a volume. He holds 12 gold discs, a Grammy for the Best Country Male Voice Performance, and was voted CMA Entertainer of the Year in 1971. He's had more than 50 singles to

his credit, with 32 of them reaching the No 1 spot in the charts, His hits include *Does My Ring Hurt Your Finger, Crystal Chandeliers, Is Anybody Goin' to San Antone,* and *Kiss an Angel Good Morning*.

Charley has been criticized by a few prejudiced whites, and by some blacks who have called him an Uncle Tom. But Charley claims with justification that he is merely an American singing American music.

Real-life songs

Son of a preacher, Tom T Hall, The Poet of Nashville, hails from Olive Hill, Kentucky. In his teens he formed a group called The Kentucky Travelers, which played for peanuts on the local radio station. After the group disbanded, Tom joined the Army and did some deejaying on AFN in Germany. Back in the States, Tom continued his disc jockey career and did his best to hawk some of his highly original compositions. His sun began to rise in 1963 when Jimmy Newman recorded his *DJ for a Day*. A year later Dave Dudley provided further encouragement with his recording of *Mad*. But Tom finally hit gold with *Harper Valley PTA*, which shot Jeannie C Riley to stardom in 1968 and sold in the millions.

When he saw that his songs could make others famous, Tom decided to record some himself. In spite of a somewhat indifferent singing voice, he broke into the Top 10 in 1968 with *Ballad of Forty Dollars*, and the following year reached No 1 with *A Week in a County Jail*. Among many other chart successes were *Old Dogs, Children, and Watermelon Vine* in 1972, *You Show Me Your Heart* in 1979, and *Everything from Jesus to Jack Daniels* in 1983.

The basis of Tom's success seems to be a carefully nurtured talent for crafting musical stories from incidents in everyday life – a talent that has reached the heart of today's country music audiences.

Transatlantic Billie Jo

Billie Jo Spears recorded her first song, *Too Old for Toys, Too Young for Boys* at the age of 13, but it was to be

Above and facing page: *Don Williams, the Gentle Giant of Country Music, was born in Plainview, Texas, and grew up in and around Corpus Christi. During his steady progress up the ladder to stardom, he had substantial hits with* The Shelter of Your Eyes *(1972),* Amanda *(1972),* 'Til the Rivers All Run Dry *(1976),* Tulsa Time *(1978), and* I Believe in You *(1980). But his warm personality is best projected on stage, where his simple guitar accompaniment, backing a quiet, easeful voice, immediately evokes such a warm response from the audience that they find themselves irresistibly joining in with the song.*

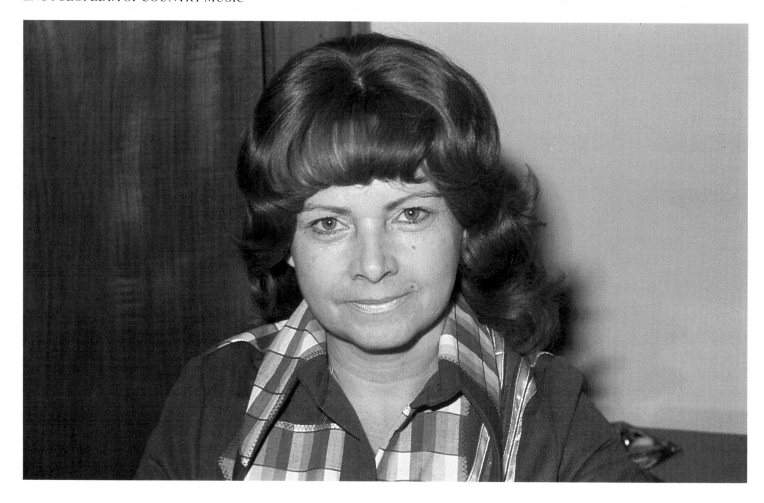

many more years before she made any significant recording impact. After leaving school she worked at several jobs but never deserted her singing and songwriting. It all eventually paid off in 1975 with *Blanket on the Ground*, a song she abhorred at first hearing. Nevertheless, she soon grew to like it, especially after it reached No 1 in the US charts and sold a quarter of a million in the UK pop charts. Once the floodgates were opened, there was no holding her. Hit followed hit, including *What I've Got in Mind*, *Sing Me an Old-Fashioned Song*, *57 Chevrolet*, and *Lonely Hearts Club*. Repeated tours nationwide and abroad brought her an international following, especially in Britain, where her bluesy, somewhat earthy voice worked like a charm.

Conway comes over to country . . .
The man who has notched up more country No 1 singles than anybody else in the business (49 by 1985) started out purely as a rock star. Conway Twitty (real name Harold Lloyd

Jenkins) was born in Friars Point, Mississippi. Just as in the case of Charley Pride, Jim Reeves, and others, baseball was the lure in Conway's life – music was merely a hobby. But after a spell in the Army, Conway was inspired to start a group of his own, when he heard Presley and Carl Perkins singing in what was then a new style.

After some time playing night clubs in rockabilly fashion, writing incessantly, and making demo recordings, Harold Jenkins changed his name to Conway Twitty, taking it from two townships in Arkansas and Texas, respectively. He took his group up to Hamilton, Ontario, where his rock show was a sellout every night for 18 consecutive weeks. It was during that period (1958) that he wrote *It's Only Make Believe*, which eventually became by far his biggest hit, selling in the millions.

In 1966, Conway moved to Nashville and eventually had two No 1 hits, *I Love You More Today* and *To See My*

Angel Cry. Then, after selling more than 16 million rock records, Conway decided that his heart was with country music after all. He came up with more hits, *Next in Line*, *Hello Darlin'*, and *15 Years Ago*, followed in 1973 by the suggestive *You've Never Been This Far Before*. Conway also teamed up with Loretta Lynn to produce probably the hottest duo in country music. Among their successes were *After the Fire Is Gone*, *Lead Me On*, and *Mississippi Woman, Louisiana Man*.

In the early 1980s Conway invested some of his millions in Twitty City, Tennessee, a complex for country music fans built around the Twitty home and office, and a Twitty showcase operated by audiovisual means.

. . . and so does Charlie Rich
Another rockabilly star of the 1950s who took the country music field by storm some 20 years later was Charlie Rich, the Silver Fox. Charlie was born in Colt, Arkansas, and his early years were dominated by religious music and jazz. He soon learnt to play sax-

Facing page: *Billie Jo Spears, a native of Texas, made her first record,* Too Old for Toys, Too Young for Boys, *at age 13. Her first entry into the charts came in 1969 with* Mr Walker It's All Over. *Her slightly honky tonky, bluesy delivery served her well with* Blanket on the Ground, *which made No 1 in 1975. Later, her international reputation expanded with offerings such as* Silver Wings and Golden Rings *and* What I've Got in Mind.

Left: *Conway Twitty, son of a riverboat captain, had a huge rock success in 1958 with* It's Only Make Believe. *From the mid-1960s onwards he began to score heavily in the country charts with his own singles and also with award-winning duets with Loretta Lynn.*

Below: *Charlie Rich, the Silver Fox, was until the 1970s a rockabilly star. Early in his career he worked with small jazz outfits and groups of bluesmen, and later formed his own jazz combo. Outstanding among his crossover hits was* Behind Closed Doors.

ophone and piano and later worked locally with small jazz combos. He studied musical theory at university, joined the Air Force, and later formed a jazz band, The Velvetones, with his wife Margaret doing the vocals.

After a spell in Memphis trying desperately to make it as a rock 'n' roller, Charlie turned to songwriting and session work. In 1959 his recording of *Lonely Weekends*, a self-penned composition, went straight into the charts and sold half a million. The song was a unique blend of rock and jazz with country overtones. Charlie persisted with this blend of styles which were evident in releases such as *Big Boss Man* and *Ways of a Woman in Love*, all of them moderately successful.

Charlie's career really began to take off after joining genius producer Billy Sherrill on the Epic label in 1968. After some minor hits he moved into the Top Ten in 1972 with *I Take It On Home*, followed by *Behind Closed Doors* in 1973. Within two years this sold three million copies, and it was immediately followed by a two-million-seller, *The Most Beautiful Girl*. In 1974 came *A Very Special Love Song*, which sold a mere million. From then on, Charlie could do no wrong in crossover terms, although country traditionalists maintained that his easy, bluesy blend of popular music was an ennervating influence on country music proper.

Gospellin' Gatlin
Larry Gatlin's early life was deeply involved with music and religion. Born in Seminole, Texas, Larry and his two brothers, Steve and Rudy, formed a gospel group when they were very young, and after winning a talent contest, gained a weekly TV series in Abilene. Later, while Larry was at the University of Houston with a career in law in mind, he was invited to join The Imperials gospel quartet. While working with them in Las Vegas he met Dottie West who recorded two of his songs, *You're the Other Half of Me* and *Once You Are Mine*. She encouraged Larry to go to Nashville and there he found generous help from Johnny Cash and Kris Kristofferson.

Larry Gatlin is the eldest of three brothers (the others being Steve and Rudy). At a crucial stage in his career he met Dottie West, who encouraged him to persist with his songwriting instead of pursuing his law studies. As a result, his songs were eventually recorded by artists such as Elvis Presley, Johnny Cash, and Tammy Wynette. He also branched out into performance, and he and his brothers are now a much in-demand group.

As a result, he recorded an album — *The Pilgrim* — for Monument in 1974. Johnny Cash also used several of his songs in the movie *The Gospel Road*.

Larry's *Broken Lady* won the Grammy Award for the best song of 1975, and he followed this a year later with another success, *Statues Without Hearts*. In 1977 came *I Just Wish You Were Someone I Love*, his first chart-topper. Another of Larry's songs, *Help Me*, appealed to several top artists, who promptly recorded it, including a moving effort by Kristofferson. Lyrics and tunes are beautifully matched in most of Larry's compositions, and in performance his tightly knit, soaring harmonies with his brothers have assured him of a loyal following through the 1980s.

Tanya Tucker

A meteoric rise to fame in the mid-1970s was achieved by Tanya Tucker, who reached the very top of the tree at the age of 14. Born in Seminole, Texas, Tanya had set her heart on being a country singer by the time she was six. Her father aided and abetted this ambition from then on. Moves for the whole family were frequent as they chased that elusive fame. Wilcox and Phoenix, Arizona, Las Vegas and Nashville were just some of the locations they haunted in an effort to persuade agents, record companies, and established stars that Tanya's demos were worth more than a cursory listen.

Finally some of her tapes landed on Billy Sherrill's Nashville desk. He was so smitten that he flew to Las Vegas to see Tanya. As a result, she landed her first recording contract and made her debut with Alex Harvey's somewhat raunchy *Delta Dawn*. Tanya's treatment of it, with her powerful, lusty, jazz-flavored voice, beat out all opposition and sent the song racing up the charts in 1972. Tanya went on to sign a million-dollar contract at age 16 and came up with equally provocative offerings such as *Would You Lay with Me in a Field of Stone* (1974), *The Man That Turned My Mama On* (1974), and *Lizzie and the Rainman* (1975). Her voice continued

Facing page and below: *Tanya Tucker hit the musical 1970s as a teenage tornado. Emerging in the 1960s from Phoenix, Arizona, she had already determined to become a top performer from the age of 8. In 1972 her recording of* Delta Dawn *made the Top Ten. There followed a string of hits including* What's Your Mama's Name?, Blood Red and Goin' Down, *and the controversial and ungrammatical* Would You Lay with Me in a Field of Stone, *which became an international hit. By that time, Tanya was earning herself a Lolita-like reputation for the suggestive content of her lyrics, but undeterred she pressed on with more country and pop winners such as* San Antone Stroll *and* Lizzie and the Rainman, *both released in 1975. Regrettably, after leaving Columbia and the guidance of producer Billy Sherrill, she abandoned her country image and style in favor of pure rock.*

Above: *Ronnie Milsap, blind from birth, was raised as a classical musician, but early in his life had formed his own rock group. He first made the charts with the rhythm 'n' blues number,* Never Had It So Good, *in 1965. Named CMA Entertainer of the Year in 1977, and the recipient of a couple of Grammy awards, Ronnie has steered a somewhat erratic course between country and pop. Among his No 1 hits were* Pure Love *(1974),* Legend in My Time *(1974), and* Why Don't You Spend the Night *(1980).*

Facing page, left: *Melba Montgomery, singer, guitarist, and fiddle player, won a talent contest in 1958 that gained her a place in Roy Acuff's band, The Smokey Mountain Boys. Later she went solo, and in 1963 came her first hit,* Hall of Shame. *Besides her solo work, she teamed up with various male artists to score hits on record. Among them were* We Must Have Been Out of Our Minds, *with George Jones, and later successes with Gene Pitney.*

Facing page, right: *Ray Stevens (born Ray Ragsdale) can be classified as a complete entertainer – a master of many instruments, singer, and composer of novelty songs and country music. Among his humorous offerings were* Ahab the Arab, Harry the Hairy Ape, *and* The Streak. *His less lunatic country hits include* Turn Your Radio On, Nashville, *and* Misty, *with its bluegrass overtones.*

to belie her tender years, and also appealed widely to the pop market. But by the 1980s she seemed to lose her interest in country music and had turned uncompromisingly to rock.

Ronnie Milsap

One of the top crossover artists is blind multi-instrumentalist Ronnie Milsap. Born in Robbinsville, North Carolina, and blind from birth, Ronnie attended a school for the blind in Raleigh, NC. There he was taught classical music and his prodigality soon showed itself in his early mastery of a variety of instruments – violin, keyboard, guitar, percussion, and woodwind. While still at school he formed a quartet, The Apparitions, that played blues, jazz, rock, and country music. Despite taking a pre-law course in Atlanta and winning a scholarship in the process, he eventually dropped out to concentrate on music.

In 1966 Ronnie formed his own professional band, which played country, jazz, R & B, and did the circuits around Memphis, Tennessee. He first

hit the charts with an R & B number, *Never Had It So Good* for Scepter in 1965. Jack D Johnson, who had initially managed Charley Pride, took him over and pushed him into the Top 10 with his first country release, *I Hate You* (1973). He reached the No 1 spot in 1974 with *Pure Love*, his third single. More success came his way with *Legend in My Time* (1974) and *Why Don't You Spend the Night* (1980).

As a country singer, Ronnie has an impressive 20 No 1 singles to his credit. He won the CMA Entertainer of the Year Award in 1977 and also won two Grammy Awards. But from the 1980s onwards he began to search for that elusive label, 'the complete entertainer', and as a result, his offerings have become more and more pop-oriented. He backed hits such as *It's All I Can Do* and *Too Big for Words* with lush strings and synthesizers, and relied heavily on sound engineers for the up-tempo treatment he needed.

Two gospel quartets

The Oak Ridge Boys began as a gospel music quartet, based on the Oak

Right: *Tom T Hall, hailing from Kentucky, has been one of the most original songwriters to grace the Nashville scene. His best known hit was* Harper Valley PTA *in 1968, which also made a star out of Jeannie C Riley, who recorded it. Tom also performs with his band, the Storytellers.*

Below: *Anne Murray, from Nova Scotia, has had some country successes, but her best numbers are crossover items. She came into prominence in 1970 with* Snowbird, *which sold a million copies or more. Over a period of eight years she managed to enter the country charts about 20 times.*

Ridge Quartet who used to entertain the workers at the Atomic Energy plant in Oak Ridge, Tennessee, during World War II. William Lee Golden, the longest serving member of the present line-up (from 1964), recruited Joe Bonsall, Richard Sterban, and Duane Allen. Their close harmony, spine-tingling singing made them one of the top gospel groups of all time. But in 1975 they moved over into country music with an impressive list of hit singles. There was *Y'All Come Back Saloon* (1977), *Leaving Louisiana in the Broad Day Light* (1979), and *American Made* (1983). But their greatest crossover hits, appealing to a wide public, were unquestionably *Elvira* (1981) and *Bobby Sue* (1982). The Oak Ridge Boys have collected a trunkful of awards along the way, including CMA Vocal Group of the Year for 1978.

An equally famous quartet, which also started out singing gospel numbers, are the so-called Statler Brothers (only two of them are brothers and nobody named Statler). They are made up of Lee DeWitt, Philip Balsley, Harold W Reid, and Don Reid, and were all childhood friends. They first began singing together in 1955, but it wasn't until Johnny Cash invited them to join his road show in 1963 that their fame began to spread. DeWitt wrote *Flowers on the Wall*, and their recording of it in 1965 became the first of many hits. Their album, *Best of the Statler Brothers*, sold well over half a million copies, and their hit singles go on and on. They include *Bed of Roses*, *Thank God I've Got You*, and *You Are My Sunshine*.

In addition to their phenomenal recording success, the Statlers also hold a July Fourth Country Musical Festival in Staunton, Virginia, at which thousands of fans turn up annually to see and hear a galaxy of stars. All profits are donated to charity – which can be counted as another laurel for the group that won the CMA Vocal Group of the Year Award for six years on the trot (1972-1977).

Melba Montgomery

Although a fine solo singer in her own

right, Melba Montgomery has tended to specialize in duets, working with, among others, Charlie Louvin, Gene Pitney, and George Jones. Born in Iron City, Tennessee, Melba's first excursion into singing was as a child in the Methodist Church at Florence, Alabama. When the family moved to Nashville in the mid-1950s, her talents so impressed Roy Acuff that he invited her to join his Smokey Mountain Boys outfit.

Melba made her solo debut in 1962 with two moderately successful singles, *Just Another Fool Along the Way* and *Happy You, Lonely Me*. In 1963 she was signed up by Pappy Daily for United Artists. It was then that she penned and recorded with George Jones her all-time bestseller, *We Must Have Been Out of Our Minds*, which won her an award for the Most Promising Singer of that year. George and Melba parted professionally in 1967, their swan song being *Party Pickin'*, but they were temporarily reunited at the 1975 Wembley Festival in London, singing together some of the old songs. In 1970 Melba teamed up with Charlie Louvin to score with numbers such as *Did You Ever* and *Something to Brag About*. In 1974 she gave notice of crossover leanings with the sentimental Harlan Howard composition *No Charge*, which not only hit the No 1 spot in the country charts but also made the pop charts. Another solo hit followed with Melba's rich Alabama voice doing full justice to *Don't Let the Good Times Fool You*.

Linda Ronstadt

Dubbed the First Lady of Country Rock, and a close friend of Dolly Parton and Emmylou Harris, is Linda Ronstadt. Born in Tucson, Arizona, Linda comes from a musical family. As a girl in Los Angeles, she formed a trio called The Stone Poneys, which recorded a few albums for Capitol. A single from one of the albums, *Different Drum*, hit the charts and gave promise of things to come. In 1969 Linda had her first solo album, *Hand Sewn, Home Grown*, soon to be followed by a second, *Silk Purse*. The latter included her first hit single,

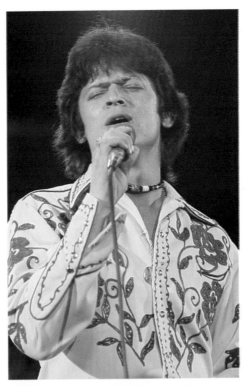

Left: *A champion of the Tex-Mex sound is Johnny Rodriguez, a young man from the Texas/Mexico border. Discovered by Bobby Bare and Tom T Hall, he hit the Top Ten with* Pass Me By *in 1972, and within the next year had three times reached No 1. A 1983 hit was* How Could I Love Her So Much.

Below: *John Denver, a middle-of-the-road balladeer, has an enormous following on both sides of the Atlantic. He won a platinum disc for his* Rocky Mountain High, *and his self-penned* Take Me Home Country Roads *and* Annie's Song *have both been recorded by very many artists.*

159

Facing page: *Crystal Gayle, younger sister of Loretta Lynn, joined her sister's road show at age 16. Her first chart release came in 1970 with* I Cried the Blue Right Out of My Eyes. *She had a greater hit in 1977 with* Don't It Make My Brown Eyes Blue, *but her later efforts had less of a country flavor and inclined more to pop.*

Below: *Linda Ronstadt deserted her home in Tucson, Arizona, and moved to Los Angeles as soon as she decently could (age 18). There she formed a trio with two men friends and they called themselves the Stone Poneys. In 1969 she decided to go solo, singing mostly rock music. After several albums, such as* Linda Ronstadt *and* Heart Like a Wheel, *her success earned her the title of Queen of Country Rock. Although she prefers not to be classed as a country singer, she likes the kinds of songs sung by Hank Williams and the Everly Brothers.*

Long Long Time. In her third album, *Linda Ronstadt,* she collaborated with three musicians who were later to form their own famous band, The Eagles. *Heart Like a Wheel* (1975), her last album for Capitol, went to No 1 in the LP charts and included a hit single *You're No Good.* In 1976 her album *Prisoner in Disguise* included a massive-selling single, *Heat Wave.* In 1977 Linda was featured on the covers of *Time, Rolling Stone,* and other magazines, and her LP *Simple Dreams* was received with universal acclaim, selling in the millions.

Going into the 1980s, Linda widened her appeal by lending her cool, uninhibited singing style more and more to rock numbers.

Little sister

Crystal Gayle has had two things going for her that marked her out from other country artistes – she has the longest hair in the business, long enough to sit on, and she is the younger sister of Loretta Lynn (although that may eventually have been a handicap). Born Brenda Gayle Webb in Paintsville, Kentucky, Crystal was the youngest of eight children and grew up in more comfortable circumstances than her famous elder sister (there is an age gap of 16 years).

For her first few professional years, Crystal worked very much in the shadow of her sister, forming part of Loretta's stage show. She had a chart entry in 1970 with a song penned by Loretta, *I Cried the Blue Right Out of My Eyes,* but it was only after signing for United Artists and going her own way under the guidance of Allen Reynolds that Crystal's career really took off. It started with a hit single, *Restless* and *Wrong Road Again,* both included in an impressive album, *Crystal Gayle* (1974). Her first No 1 single was *I'll Get Over You* (1976), but her smash hit was *Don't It Make My Brown Eyes Blue* (1977), which not

only made her the darling of the pop fans but also won her awards from the CMA and the Academy of Country Music. Further evidence of Crystal's love affair with pop was her album *We Must Believe in Magic* and her 1982 duet with Eddie Rabbitt, *You and I.*

Anne Murray

Canadian songstress Anne Murray found herself a country star more or less by accident. Born in Springhill, Nova Scotia, Anne's musical upbringing was on the classical side. She graduated as a physical education teacher and at that time her feelings about country music were hazily pejorative. But, needing the money for a car, she auditioned for a Canadian TV series and was accepted. Capitol Records, intrigued by her musical, slightly husky voice, signed her up, and in 1970 she emerged with her version of Gene McClelland's *Snowbird*. It went to No 1, sold more than a million copies, and established Anne as an international star in both country and pop fields. With some 20 entries in the country charts over the following nine years, Anne moved steadily on, but from 1978 onwards she moved into another gear, leaning heavily on pop-oriented numbers. They included hits such as *You Needed Me* (1978), *Broken-Hearted Me* (1979), and *Could I Have This Dance* (1980).

Spanish Country Sound

Johnny Rodriguez, The First Chicano of Country Music, as he has been called, was born Juan Raul Davis Rodriguez in the little township of Sabinal, Texas, about 90 miles from the Mexican border. His fairy story rise to fame is the stuff of legends. Driven by hunger to rustle and barbecue a goat in a Texas park, he was subsequently jailed. A benevolent Texas Ranger, Joaquin Jackson, heard him playing guitar and singing in his cell, and found him a job with 'Happy' Shahan, whose tourist attraction was located at Alamo Village. Tom T Hall and Bobby Bare heard Johnny sing there and eventually enticed him to Nashville. There he joined The Storytellers, Tom's band, as a guitarist, and later signed a contract with Mercury.

Facing page: *Besides being a successful singer, Lynn Anderson is also an expert horserider, with many trophies to prove it. The song she will be remembered most for was* Rose Garden, *released in 1970. This massive international hit gained her the CMA Female Singer of the Year Award, and ensured that many of her subsequent recordings entered the country charts.*

Left: *Singer/songwriter Mel Tillis turned a potentially ruinous stutter into a profitable comic trademark. His audiences have come to expect and love it. A signal success was his composition* Detroit City, *made famous by Bobby Bare.*

Below: *Hoyt Axton, originally a folk singer, eventually became a highly sought after country music writer. Among his many hits were* Greenback Dollar, The Pusher, *and* Snowblind Friend. *He also made successful appearances in TV movies.*

Johnny's first single, *Pass Me By* (1972) made the charts, and within a year he had notched up three No 1s – *You Always Come Back*, *Ridin' My Thumb to Mexico*, and *That's the Way Love Goes*. Johnny's intriguing Tex-Mex style, with occasional interjections in Spanish in mid-song, has endeared him to a wide audience, and his chart appearances continued into the 1980s, with *How Could I Love Her So Much* scoring particularly heavily in 1983.

Roy's country songs

Roy Clark has been called the Compleat Entertainer, a description that could be an understatement. It would be difficult to list all of his talents, features, and attributes. but here are some of them: singer, songwriter, master showman and multi-instrumentalist (guitar, banjo, fiddle, piano, trombone, trumpet, accordion and drums), comedian, photographer, champion boxer, broadcaster, boat captain, horse breeder, rancher, pilot, and president of a diet food chain. Roy Linwood Clark was born in Meherrin, Virginia, and started on the banjo at age three. By the time he was 16 he had won the national Country Music Banjo Championship two years in succession. At 14 he was playing guitar for local square dances.

Roy's professional career started as a back-up musician in the 1950s and 1960s for some of the top stars of the time – George Hamilton IV, Wanda Jackson, Marvin Rainwater. He entered the charts for the first time on Capitol in 1963 with *Tips of My Fingers*. After numerous TV appearances and cabaret concerts in the 1960s, Roy achieved national fame with his interpretation of Charles Aznavour's *Yesterday When I Was Young*. Recorded on Dot Records in 1969 it broke through to the pop charts. He went on to make a number of country recordings, including *Come Live with Me* (1973) and *If I Had to Do It All Over Again* (1976), and demonstrated his vast versatility by playing classical, bluegrass, jazz, and pop in sessions at home and abroad.

This versatility has shown itself in

Facing page, top: *Richard 'Kinky' Friedman was leader of a way out country rock band, the Texas Jewboys, whose main claim to fame rests on their 1973 album,* Sold American.

Facing page, bottom: *A master of many instruments, singer, comedian, and entertainer, Roy Clark is one of the outstanding stars of the TV show Hee-Haw.*

Below: *The Statler Brothers, made up of Lew De Witt, Philip Balsley, Harold Reid and Don Reid, were voted CMA Vocal Group of the Year for many years in succession. Originally known as the Kingsmen, they changed their name to the present one when they joined the Johnny Cash road show in 1963. Among their many hits have been* I'll Go to My Grave Loving You, I Was There, *and* You Are My Sunshine.

The talented Mandrell Sisters, Louise and
Irlene, were eyecatchingly headed by Barbara,
singer and multi-instrumentalist, in their own
TV series for a couple of seasons. Barbara was
uniquely twice winner of the CMA Entertainer of
the Year award. In 1984 she was severely injured
in a car crash.

his co-hosting of the enormously successful TV show Hee-Haw from its inception in 1969, his participation in the Montreux Jazz Festival, his visit to Moscow with his road show (the first country music artist to do so), and his 1973 CMA Award as Entertainer of the Year. And yet, in spite of having recorded more than 40 LPs, he loses something on disc – the real Roy Clark can only be appreciated to the full in a live performance.

A headful of dreams

That walking, singing, playing contradiction, John Denver, with his sugar-sweet, healthy, outdoor, all-American boy image, has been variously dubbed as dealing in country, pop, and easy-listening middle-of-the-road music. Born Henry John Deutschendorf in Roswell, New Mexico, he later moved to Colorado and from then on never ceased to sing the praises of his adopted state. John early became an adept picker on an old Gibson guitar, and at first was attracted to rock 'n' roll, then to folk music. In 1965 he replaced Chad Mitchell in the trio of that name, and worked with them until 1969. In that year he decided to go solo, recording for Victor.

John's first hit was his self-penned folk song, *Leaving on a Jet Plane*. It was recorded by Peter, Paul and Mary and won a gold disc. Other artists began to notice and record John's compositions, and he returned the compliment by singing material penned by such stalwarts as Tom Paxton, Lennon and McCartney, and James Taylor. Almost all of John's albums have gained gold or platinum status, including *Poems, Prayers and Promises*, and *Rocky Mountain High*. In 1971 his *Take Me Home Again, Country Roads* was played and recorded in the pop

field more than on the strictly country circuit. John's unashamedly romantic views of rural life met an enthusiastic response from urban teenagers, and he went on to record hits such as the wildly successful *Annie's Song* (1974) and *Back Home Again* (1974). He was also heard with Emmylou Harris in *Wild Mountain Skies* (1983), and even attempted duets with international opera star Placido Domingo in 1984.

Kenny Rogers studied music and commercial art before becoming one of the New Christy Minstrels. In 1967 he formed another popular group, The First Edition, whose hits included Just Dropped In, Ruby Don't Take Your Love to Town, *and* Tell It All, Brother. *After going solo, he came up with a massive hit in 1977,* Lucille, *which attained the No 1 position in the country charts and also made great inroads into the pop field. He later teamed up with Dottie West in a fruitful partnership that yielded hits such as* All I Ever Needed Is You.

Rick Nelson was early exposed to the footlights' glare because his parents were themselves radio and TV performers. In the late 1950s he was a confirmed and locally idolized pop star. The advent of the Beatles swept him into temporary limbo, along with many others. But in 1967 he turned up again, this time as one of the pioneer country rockers. The immediate results were two moderately successful albums, Country Fever and Bright Lights and Country Music. He went on tour in 1969 with a country rock band, the Stone Canyon Band. He later wrote Garden Party, a poignant piece of autobiography about his being booed off the stage at Madison Square Garden. Consolingly, it earned him a gold disc.

Right: Moe Bandy and Joe Stampley get to grips with things. Ex-rodeo rider Moe Bandy boasts of being 'solidly country', a claim that's certainly borne out by his modern treatment of traditional honky tonk slippin' around songs. In the 1970s he joined forces with Joe Stampley, an ex-pop star turned country artist, to produce the hit, Just Good Ol' Boys.

Right, below, and facing page: *There have been a few moderately successful black country singers, but the only true superstar has been Charley Pride. With more than 50 hit singles and a dozen gold discs to his credit, he can certainly claim to have integrated country music. RCA were at first worried that there might be trouble with his records in the racially sensitive areas of the South. In the event, they need not have worried – Charley sold more of their records than any other artist except Elvis Presley.*

8

Who's Who
& Index

Ricky Skaggs, CMA Male Vocalist award winner, owes much to his bluegrass roots. He has developed from a child prodigy into a master instrumentalist.

Note: Numbers in *italics* refer to pictures.

Acuff, Roy Claxton (1903-) Famous oldtime fiddler/singer who formed a link between hillbilly music and modern commercial sounds. With his group, The Smokey Mountain Boys, recorded country music classics such as *Great Speckled Bird* and *Wabash Cannonball* 16, 31, 32, 43-46, *46, 47*

Adcock, Eddie Way out bluegrass banjo player. *See* COUNTRY GENTLEMEN

Addington, Maybelle. *See* CARTER, 'Mother' Maybelle

Akeman, David. *See* STRINGBEAN

Allen, Rex (1924-) The 'Arizona Cowboy' was originally a rodeo rider who became last of the singing cowboys in the movies. Best known records include *Money, Marbles and Chalk* and *Crying in the Chapel* 59, *59*, 60

Anderson, Bill (1937-) Prolific songwriter and performer, 'Whispering Bill' has written more than 1,000 songs. First big hit was *City Lights* (1958), with which Ray Price earned a golden disc 124

Anderson, Lynn (1947-) Crossover artist whose jackpot hit, *Rose Garden* (1970), soared to No 1 in the country and pop charts in many countries, and won her a gold disc and a Grammy award *162*

Arizona Cowboy. *See* ALLEN, Rex

Arnold, Eddy (Richard Edward) [1918-] One of the most influential country music performers during 40 years, the 'Tennessee Plowboy' with the commercial crooning voice has sold about 70 million discs, including *Bouquet of Roses* and *Make the World Go Away* 88, 89, *130*

Ashley, Clarence 'Tom' (1895-1967)

Born Clarence Earl McCurry, Ashley was a fine early mountain banjoist and guitarist. A founder member of the Carolina Tar Heels, he made a comeback in the 1960s, recording *Music at Clarence Ashley's, Volumes I and II* 15, 16

Atkins, 'Chet' (Chester Burton) [1924-] Originally a top session guitarist, he became a vice-president of RCA and helped to establish the 'Nashville sound'. Voted Best Instrumentalist for 14 years in succession, his hits include *Poor People of Paris* and *Yakety Axe* *110-111*, 111, 112, 148

Autry, Orvon Gene (1907-) Most famous of the screen's singing cowboys, he made innumerable B Westerns with his horse, Champion. His *Silver-Haired Daddy of Mine* sold more than 5 million copies, only exceeded by his *Rudolph the Red-Nosed Reindeer* with 10 million 21, 48-56, *49, 50, 51, 53, 54*

Axton, Hoyt (1932-) Originally a folk singer, he had a huge hit in 1979 with *Della and the Dealer* 163

Baez, Joan (1941-) Nonviolent protest singer/songwriter, author, and guitarist, she has been in the forefront of activist demonstrations and folk get-togethers for many years, enlivening the scene with her moving singing and impassioned sincerity 15

Bailey, DeFord (1899-) First black musician to appear on the Grand Ole Opry, he went on stage in 1927 at the impromptu christening of the show by George Hay. Bailey's limited repertoire

on the harmonica included *Pan American Blues* and *John Henry* 7, 32, 148

Baker, Bob Tall, gangling, baby-faced movie cowboy from Colorado whose 1930s films, constantly under-financed, eventually faded him from the screen 54

Bandy, Moe (1944-) Former rodeo-rider and sheet-metal worker, he became one of the luminaries of the hardcore honky tonk style in the early 1970s. Hits include *I Just Started Hatin' Cheatin' Songs Today* and *Hank Williams, You Wrote My Life* 136-138, *169*

Bare, Bobby (1935-) Shrewd, talented, ever popular songwriter and performer, his first hit was *All American Boy*, recorded under the name of Bill Parsons in 1958. After army service he returned with *Detroit City*, which sold a million. The whole Bare family appeared on his 1976 album hit *Singin' in the Kitchen* 124-6, *124*

Bate, Alcyone. Daughter of Dr Humphry Bate. *See* BATE, Dr Humphry

Bate, Dr Humphry (1875-1936) A practicing physician, Dr Bate played the harmonica for his band, The Possum Hunters, the most popular string band ever to appear on the Opry. First broadcast on Nashville radio in 1925 *28-9*, 29

Birchfield, Benny Bluegrass guitarist and harmony singer. *See* OSBORNE BROTHERS

Blackwood Brothers Arguably the world's most famous gospel group, they have sold about 17 million discs over their 36 years of public performance. Their No 1 song, *Learning to Lean*, was in the Top 40 for a record 15 consecutive months 80-1, 94

bluegrass Lively development of oldtime string band music, pioneered by Bill Monroe, and owing much of its

Chet Atkins

exciting sound to the driving rhythm of the 5-string banjo. Has been described as 'folk song with overdrive' *66-78*

Blue Ridge Playboys Influential western swing band of the 1930s whose various members later disbanded to pioneer the first honky tonk outfits *64*

Blue Sky Boys Born Bill (1917-) and Earl (1919-) Bolick, a singing duo highly influential in the formative years of bluegrass, with their close harmony treatment of traditional material. First release (1936) was *The Sunny Side of Life* *38*, 41-2, 43, *45*

Boggs, Dock (1898-) Traditional singer and gifted banjoist of the late 1920s. His wife frowned on his 'sinful' banjo playing, so he went down the mines for half a century before being musically discovered by Mike Seeger in the 1960s *35*

Bolick Brothers. *See* BLUE SKY BOYS

Bond, Johnny (1915-) Singing cowboy film star, for 30 years associated with Gene Autry. Composed more than 500 songs, including *Cimarron* and *I Wonder Where You Are Tonight* *59*

Boxcar Willie (1932-) Singer/ songwriter (Lecil Travis Martin) who built up a popular following by appearing on stage dressed as a bum and performing underplayed renditions of Hank Williams, Jimmie Rodgers, and self-penned railroad material, punctuated with lifelike train whistle sounds *132, 136*

Boyd, Bill Texas cowboy film star of the 1930s who sang to his own guitar accompaniment and headed a band called the Cowboy Ramblers *64*

Brockman, Polk C Atlanta distributor for the Victor record company. *See* CARSON, Fiddlin' John; PEER, Ralph Sylvester

Brown, Milton (1903-36) Pioneer of western swing and one-time member of the Light Crust Doughboys. His later band, the Music Brownies, recorded hits such as *The Wheel of the Wagon Is Broken* *60*

Buckaroos, The. *See* OWENS, Buck

Burnett, Dick (1883-1954) Blinded by a mugger early in life, banjoist and multi-instrumentalist Burnett later teamed up with singing fiddler Leonard Rutherford to become the first duo to record pre-guitar mountain music *15*

Burns, Kenneth C. *See* HOMER AND JETHRO

C

Callahan Brothers Walter T 'Joe' (1910-) and Homer C 'Bill' (1912-71) were popular radio and recording stars of the 1930s. Their later material was mostly western swing *33, 36*

Campbell, Glen (1936-) Singer/ songwriter, multi-instrumentalist, and in-demand session guitarist who in the 1980s became one of the hottest properties in country and crossover pop music. Among dozens of his hits were *Galveston* and *By the Time I Get to Phoenix* 141-2, *145*

Cannon, Sarah. *See* PEARL, Minnie

Carlisle Brothers Cliff (1904-) and Bill (1908-), popular, long-serving guitar and dobro duo who abandoned traditional close harmony duets for wilder singing mixed with yodels and comedy *33, 36-38*

Carolina Tar Heels Early string band originally made up of Clarence Ashley (guitar), Dock Walsh (banjo), and Garley Foster (guitar and harmonica). All three were vocal and instrumental soloists in their own right and recorded many hits for Victor from 1928 onwards *15*

Carson, Fiddlin' John (1868-1949) Oldtime Georgia fiddler who in 1923 made the first commercial recording of a country song. The two sides were *The Little Old Cabin in the Lane* and *The Old Hen Cackled and the Rooster's Going to Crow.* It was recorded for Ralph Peer *7, 9*

Carter, Alvin Pleasant Delaney (1891-1960) Famed founder and leader of the Carter Family trio. Sang bass with wife Sara and sister-in-law Maybelle. Collected traditional material and claimed much of it as his own, after reworking 21-25, *22*, 35, 80

Carter, June (1929-) Daughter of Maybelle, June first sang with her sisters but later went solo successfully, co-writing *Ring of Fire.* Started touring with Johnny Cash in 1967, their big hit being *Jackson.* Became Mrs Cash in 1968 25, 104, 106, *128*

Carter, 'Mother' Maybelle (1909-78) Born Maybelle Addington, she married A P Carter's brother Ezra in 1926 and formed part of the Carter Family trio. Sang alto-harmony, played autoharp and banjo, and initiated a much copied country 'lick' on guitar 21-25, *21*, 46

Carter, Sara (1898-1979) Born Sara Dougherty, she was one of the singing and playing trio that made up the Carter Family. She married A P Carter in 1915. In the group she sang a strong lead and played guitar and autoharp. Divorced in 1938, she married Coy Bayes a year later but did little professional work after 1941 21-25, *22*

Carter Family Regarded as the original country music family, they consisted of A P Carter, his wife Sara, and sister-in-law Maybelle. They were recorded for the first time by Ralph Peer in 1927, and among the six songs were *The Storms Are on the Ocean* and *Little Log Cabin by the Sea* 16, 21-25, *22*, 35, 80

Cash, Johnny (1932-) World's best known country singer; came from an underprivileged background to make good with Luther Perkins and Marshall Grant. Constant tours and unceasing work brought on exhaustion and an

Maybelle Carter

addiction to pills. June Carter, his second wife, did much to rehabilitate him. Hits include **Folsom Prison Blues** 25, 104-09, *105*, 141

Choates, Harry (1926-51) Cajun fiddler whose 1946 hit, **Jole Blon,** was variously recorded way beyond the limits of Cajun. Choates expired in an Austin jail after a short, wild, alcoholic career 82

Chuck Wagon Gang Gospel group formed in 1933, made up of D P (Dad) Carter and three of his offspring – Rose, Anna, and Ernest. They relied on acoustic strings (guitars, mandolin, etc) and operated for years around the Fort Worth area 80

Clark, Roy Linwood (1933-) Talented multi-instrumentalist and comedian, he is known as the complete entertainer. Star of the TV show Hee-Haw, he won the CMA Entertainer of the Year award in 1973 *164,* 165

Clifton, Bill (1931-) Ex-Marine officer and Peace Corps member, Bill sings, plays guitar and autoharp, and spreads the good news of bluegrass over many parts of the globe. Has recorded with most of the bluegrass greats and leans heavily on Carter Family and similar material *73,* 75

Clinch Mountain Boys Oldtime string band formed by the Stanley Brothers in 1946. *See* STANLEY BROTHERS

Cline, Patsy (1932-63) Born Virginia Patterson Hensley, she shared with Kitty Wells the title of 'Queen of Country Music'. First hit was **Walking After Midnight** (1957), followed by many more. She was killed in an airplane crash along with Hawkshaw Hawkins and Cowboy Copas *36,* 121

Colley, Sarah Ophelia. *See* PEARL, Minnie

Colter, Jessi (1947-) Born Miriam Johnson, she adopted her stage name from distantly related outlaw Jesse Colter. Twice married (Duane Eddy, Waylon Jennings), she wrote and performed her greatest hit, **I'm Not Lisa** in 1975 *140,* 141

Cooley, Spade (Donell C) [1910-69] King of western swing in the 1940s, he led a sometimes huge band performing on fiddle and playing a mixture of jazz, blues, and dance music. Jailed for wife-slaying, he died of heart failure during temporary release 63, *64*

Copas, Lloyd 'Cowboy' (1913-63) Brought up on a ranch, he became a popular star of the 1940s with hits such as **Filipino Baby** and **Signed, Sealed and Delivered.** After a decline in his career in the 1950s, he hit the top again in 1961 with **Alabam.** In 1963 he was killed in the plane crash that also took the lives of Patsy Cline and Hawkshaw Hawkins 121

Country Gazette Originally made up of Byron Berline (fiddle), Roger Bush (string bass), Kenny Wertz (vocals, guitar), Alan Munde (vocals, banjo), and Roland White (vocals, mandolin, guitar), the group formed up from the

remains of the extinct Flying Burritos in the 1970s. Forte was uptempo bluegrass and comedy *76-7,* 78

Country Gentlemen Urban progressive bluegrass group originally consisting of Charlie Waller (guitar), John Duffy (mandolin), Eddy Adcock (banjo), and Tom Grey (bass), formed around 1957. Two hits from a wide range are **Bringing Mary Home** and **The Fields Have Turned Brown** 72

Country Music Association Organization founded in 1958 to promote country music around the world. Their annual Country Music Awards were first established in 1967

Country Music Hall of Fame and Museum Originally opened in 1967 in Nashville but remodeled and expanded in 1977, the museum and library were created by the Country Music Foundation to house books, films, musical instruments and memorabilia of country music stars *34*

Crown Prince of Country Music. *See* JONES, George

Crown Prince of Honky Tonk. *See* BANDY, Moe

Crum, Simon. *See* HUSKY, Ferlin

Johnny Cash

Jessi Colter

Patsy Cline

Daffan, Ted (Theron Eugene) [1912-] Prolific Texas singer/ songwriter/guitarist who wrote the allegedly first ever trucking song, **Truck Drivers' Blues,** in 1939. Subsequent hits included **Worried Mind** and **Born to Lose** 64

Daily, Harold W 'Pappy' (1902-) Texan record producer and successful company executive who formed Starday in the early 1950s. Among his many signings were George Jones, Gene Pitney, and Melba Montgomery 122

Dalhart, Vernon (1883-1948) Born Marion Try Slaughter, he recorded the first country record to sell a million copies, **The Wreck of the Old '97** and **The Prisoner's Song,** in 1924. Was originally a light opera singer and performer of 'coon' songs 6, 7, 8

Davis, Skeeter (1931-) Born Mary Frances Penick, early formed a duo with close friend Betty Jack Davis and called themselves the Davis Sisters. In 1953 Betty was killed and Skeeter badly hurt in a car wreck. Skeeter later continued with a successful solo career 116, 117, 117, 118, 119

Deason, Muriel. See WELLS, Kitty

Delmore Brothers Alton (1908-64) and Rabon (1910-52) were popular Opry fiddle and guitar duettists during the 1930s. Their close harmony singing and professionalism became evident in hits such as **Blues Stay Away From Me** (1949) 12, 38-9

Denver, John (1943-) Born John Henry Deutschendorf, a soft rock musician who started off as a folk singer with the Chad Mitchell Singers. Greatest hit was self-penned **Country Roads** 159, 168

Deutschendorf, John Henry. See DENVER, John

Dexter, Al (1905-) Born Albert Poindexter, he was a singer/songwriter of the 1930s and 1940s who formed the Texas Troupers. His self-penned **Pistol Packin' Mama** sold in the millions and made a packet for him and especially Bing Crosby 64

Dickens, Little Jimmy (1925-) Diminutive singing star, also known as 'Tater', who in 1965 provided both country and pop fans with the enormous hit, **May the Bird of Paradise Fly Up Your Nose** 120, 121

Dillards, The Bluegrass semi-rock band formed basically of Rodney (1942-) and Doug (1937-), who later teamed up with Mitch Jayne and Dean Webb. Later changes saw the arrival of Byron Berline and Herb Pederson. Their approach was expert but lighthearted, as can be heard in **Back Porch Bluegrass** 77, 78, 79

Dixie Clodhoppers Pioneer Opry band of the 1920s whose music, like their stage garb, was cheerful and outlandish 29

Dixieliners, The Influential 1930s fiddle band formed by Arthur Smith and the McGee brothers. See SMITH, Fiddlin' Arthur

Dougherty, Sara. See CARTER, Sara

Drifting Cowboys Band formed by Hank Williams. See WILLIAMS, Hank

Dudley, Dave (1928-) Originally a rockabilly artist, he cut **Six Days on the Road** in 1961, with nothing to show for it until two years later when it became a roaring success and set the pattern for more trucking songs such as **Truck Drivin' Son of a Gun** 126

Duffey, John Mandolin player and bluegrass virtuoso. See COUNTRY GENTLEMEN

Duncan, Tommy (1911-67) Bluesy baritone who joined the Light Crust Doughboys in 1932 and became Bob Wills' lead singer. He followed Wills into the Texas Playboys and in 1948 formed his own band, the Western All Stars 63

Eagles, The Soft rock band from the West Coast. See RONSTADT, Linda

Earl Scruggs Revue Band formed by Earl Scruggs after his split from Lester Flatt in 1969. The outfit consisted of Earl, his sons, and Josh Graves. Music was experimental and rock-orientated. See SCRUGGS, Earl 69

Evans, Dale. See ROGERS, Roy

Everly Brothers Don (1937-) and Phil (1939-) were originally country guitarists and close harmony singers who flirted for some years with rock and later returned to country music. Their first hit was **Bye Bye Love,** followed by chartbusters such as **Wake Up Little Susie** and **Bird Dog,** all meat and drink to their frenzied fans

131, 146

Flatt, Lester Raymond (1914-79) Bluegrass guitarist and one half of the world famous Flatt and Scruggs partnership. Lester and Earl parted company in 1969, with Lester forming a new group, Nashville Grass, to play traditional music 66, 68, 69, 71, 80

Foley, 'Red' (Clyde Julian) [1910-68] Opry star who devoted much of his time to performing religious songs. In the 1950s he hosted the first successful country TV series – the Ozark Jubilee 38, 64, 89, 90, 90, 101, 112

Ford, Tennessee Ernie (Ernie Jennings) [1919-] Began as a DJ in Bristol, Tennessee, but after moving to California was discovered by Cliffie Stone. His big hits were **Shotgun Boogie** and especially **Sixteen Tons** 64, 80, 102, 109, 128

Foster, Garley Guitar and harmonica player in the 1920s. See CAROLINA TAR HEELS

John Denver

Friedman, Richard 'Kinky' Controversial rock artist who called himself the Texas Jewboy. His great hit was **Sold American** (1973) 164

Frizzell, 'Lefty' (William Orville) [1928-75] Originally a boxer with a formidable left hand, he became an Opry star in the 1950s. His honky tonk style influenced many followers, including Merle Haggard 94, 95, 128

G

Gatlin, Larry (1948-) Successful singer/songwriter whose roots lay in gospel music. Discovered by Dottie West and supported by Johnny Cash and Kris Kristofferson, he produced hits such as *I Just Wish You Were Someone I Love* and *All the Gold in California* 152, *152-3*

Gayle, Crystal (1951-) Born Brenda Gayle Webb, she grew up overshadowed by her famous elder sister, Loretta Lynn. Since then she has made a successful solo career, making her debut with *I've Cried the Blue Right Out of My Eyes,* penned by Loretta 160, *161*

Gentry, Bobbie (1944-) Folk and country/pop singer who made her indelible mark with *Ode to Billy Joe* (1953). *See* CAMPBELL, Glen

Gibson, Don (1928-) Singer/songwriter with great appeal to pop as well as country fans. Was an ever present radio star in Knoxville in the 1950s. His *Oh Lonesome Me* and *I*

Can't Stop Loving You made him a rich man, especially when Ray Charles adopted the latter 121, *127*

Gilliland, Henry Oldtime fiddler who, in 1922 at the age of 74, made with Eck Robertson the first country record by country artists. *Sally Goodin* and *Arkansas Traveler* were the two tracks released 8

Glaser, Tompall (1933-) Leader and best known of the Glaser Brothers, harmony singers who peaked in the late 1950s and 1960s. Tompall left his brothers in 1973 to join 'outlaws' Waylon Jennings and Willie Nelson, but the group reformed in the 1980s

gospel music Religious celebration in song that formed part of the genesis of country music and rhythm and blues. Confined to church congregations and black plantation workers in the 1800s, it broadened its horizons via quartets and bluegrass, until today it is one of the fastest growing phenomena in American music 66-78

Grand Ole Opry Live country music radio stage show emanating from Nashville. It has had several moves in its 60-year history, and today it is housed in a purpose-built theater in Opryland park 26-47, *26, 27, 41*

Grayson, George Banman Blind fiddler, oldtime partner of Henry

Tennessee Ernie Ford

179

Whitter. *See* WHITTER, Henry

Greenbriar Boys Bluegrass band from New York, formed in 1958, originally made up of John Herald (guitar), Bob Yellin (banjo) and Eric Weissberg (banjo). Included in their expert playing and singing were many of their own compositions 77

Grey, Tom Bluegrass bass player. *See* COUNTRY GENTLEMEN

Gully Jumpers Early Opry string band made up of Bert Hutcherson (guitar), Charlie Arrington (fiddle), Paul Warmack (mandolin and guitar), and Roy Hardison (banjo). One of the most durable outfits, they survived professionally from around 1927 until the mid-1960s 29

Hackberry Ramblers Most popular Cajun band of the 1930s, did much to spread the influence of their type of music. Made up of Luderin Darbone (fiddle), Edwin Duhon (bass), and Lennis Sonnier (guitar), they sang in a curious patois and made popular such numbers as *Fais Pa Ca* 82

Haggard, Merle (1937-) Uncompromising California-based singer/songwriter who in the late 1960s created a sensation with his tongue-in-cheek, voice-of-the-silent-majority number, *Okie from Muskogee*. With his group, The Strangers, he has recorded some outstanding concept records 134-5, *135*, 136, 139

Hall, Tom T (1936-) Inventive songwriter of humorous and quirky people and situations, he has been called the Mark Twain of Country Music. His first million-seller, *Harper Valley PTA*, was made famous by Jeannie C Riley in 1968 148, *158*

Hamilton IV, George (1937-) Pleasant-voiced singer of easy listening songs, he was raised on folk and western songs. Always immaculately dressed and groomed, he is particularly popular in Britain and Canada, and has been called the 'International Ambassador of Country Music' *118*, 126-7

Harkreader, Sid Pioneer Nashville fiddler and singer. *See* MACON, Uncle Dave

Harris, Emmylou (1949-) Originally an unsuccessful folk singer, she found her niche in country rock and pop, and became known in the 1980s as the First Lady of Contemporary Country Music. Backed by her Hot Band (a hand-picked group of superb musicians), she appealed to a wide spectrum of appreciative fans 146, *147*, 168

Hart, Freddie (1933-) Ex-marine whose boyhood ambition had always been to achieve country stardom, he

finally made it with *Easy Loving*. It hit the charts in 1971 and stayed there for 24 weeks, and was also the CMA's Song of the Year for two years on the trot *126*, 128

Hay, George Dewey (1895-1968) Self-styled 'Solemn Old Judge' of the Grand Ole Opry, initiated the WSM Barn Dance in Nashville in 1925 and two years later gave it its new and everlasting name 26, *30*, 32, *39*

Haynes, Henry D. *See* HOMER AND JETHRO

Hee-Haw Syndicated TV show that popularizes country music and corny humor. It began in 1969 and featured stars such as Grandpa Jones, Roy Clark, and Buck Owens

Hensley, Virginia Patterson. *See* CLINE, Patsy

Herald, John Bluegrass guitarist. *See* GREENBRIAR BOYS

hillbilly music Epithet applied to the music provided by the earliest string bands. The description was allegedly coined by Ralph Peer in the 1920s, and later became a term of contempt 6-25

Homer and Jethro Henry D Haynes (1917-71) and Kenneth C Burns (1923-), were a comedy duo who delighted audiences from 1932 until Homer's death in 1971. Their humor

was unsophisticated, but they were gifted musicians and they recorded several parodies of contemporary country and pop hits *98*, 101, 102

honky tonk A style of country music that evolved largely from western swing and reached its peak in the 1940s. It was played loudly in roadside taverns and dealt with the realities of drinking, infidelity, and life's frustrations. Ernest Tubb, Al Dexter, and George Jones were in the forefront 64

Hot Band Backing group of Emmylou Harris. *See* HARRIS, Emmylou

Hubbard, Jerry. *See* REED, Jerry

Husky, Ferlin (1927-) Early in life worked as a DJ in California with the name of Terry Preston, which he also used on some of his records. For hayseed satire he called himself Simon Crum. First big success was a duet with Jean Shepard, *Dear John Letter* in 1953 121-22

George Dewey Hay

I

International Ambassador of Country Music. *See* HAMILTON IV, George

J

Jean, Norma. *See* WAGONER, Porter
Jenkins, Harold Lloyd. *See* TWITTY, Conway

Jenkins, Snuffy Pioneer banjoist whose three-finger roll had a strong influence on the later bluegrass styles of Earl Scruggs and Don Reno   66
Jennings, Waylon (1937-) One of the leading 'outlaws' of country music who in the late 1960s and 1970s became impatient with the material he was supposed to record. By 1972 he had secured full autonomy and began to produce records with songs by young contemporary writers   136, *137*, 138
Jim and Jesse (McReynolds) A bluegrass duo whose unique high harmonies have enchanted audiences all over the world. Jim (1927-) and Jesse (1929-) made their professional debut in 1947 and were still active in the 1980s. Jim's guitar complements some fine cross-picking on Jesse's mandolin   72, *72*
Johnson, Miriam. *See* COLTER, Jessi
Jones, George (1931-) Controversial but highly influential honky tonk singer who first charted in 1955 with **Why Baby Why**. Married Tammy Wynette in 1969 and divorced six years later. Drink, women, and debt almost ruined him, but he fought back, and now has recorded more than 100 hits   122, *123*
Jones, 'Grandpa' (Louis Marshall) [1913-] Banjo-playing, wisecracking, high kicking comedian and all-round entertainer on both the Opry and Hee-Haw. In his early twenties he hit on the gimmick of disguising himself as an old man   36, 38, *42*, 99

K

Kentucky Colonels Uptempo bluegrass group who brought new dimensions to their kind of music in the early 1970s with peerless expertise. The definitive group was made up of Clarence White (guitar), Roland White (mandolin), Roger Bush (bass), and Billy Ray Latham (banjo)   75, 77, 78
Kentucky Wonder. *See* STRINGBEAN
Kershaw, Doug and Rusty Douglas James (1936-) and his brother Russell Lee formed a duo in the 1950s playing and singing Cajun music. Their wild fiddling and exuberant singing ensured them a steady following. *Louisiana Man* and *Diggy Liggy Lo* were two favorites   *80*, 82
Kincaid, Bradley (1895-) Singer and guitarist, a popular pioneer broadcaster, and performer and collector of Kentucky mountain songs. Became known as the 'Kentucky Mountain Boy'   15, *17*
Kirby, Pete. *See* OSWALD, Bashful Brother
Kristofferson, Kris (1936-) Accomplished athlete, scholar, composer, and actor, he hit the headlines when his **Me and Bobby McGee** was recorded by Roger Miller. Johnny Cash did the same for another of his hits, **Sunday Morning Coming Down**   141, *142*, 143

L

Lewis Family Known as the 'First Family of Bluegrass Gospel Music', they have been putting religion into overdrive since the early 1950s. Originally made up of Roy (Pop) Lewis with his two sons and three daughters, all singing and playing acoustic instruments plus piano   81
Light Crust Doughboys Pioneer western swing outfit formed by Bob Wills. *See* WILLS, Bob
Locklin, Hank (Lawrence Hankins) [1918-] Singer guitarist whose perseverance paid off in the 1950s with chartbusters such as **Send Me the Pillow You Dream On** and **Please Help Me I'm Falling**. Was eventually elected mayor of his birthplace, McLellan, Florida   119
Lonzo and Oscar Stage names of the Sullivan Brothers, John (Lonzo) [1917-67] and Rollin (Oscar) [1919-]. They were an Opry comedy duo who had them rolling in the aisles for about 20 years with offerings such as *Take*

Homer

Them Cold Feet out of My Back
102, *103*

Loudermilk, John D (1934-) A gifted songwriter, this ex-Salvation Army bandsman is notoriously shy of public appearances. His catalog of hits has largely been popularized by other artists. Songs include ***Abilene, A Rose and Baby Ruth,*** and ***Language of Love*** 127, *127*

Louisiana Hayride Saturday night show from radio KWKH, Shreveport, Indiana, which started in 1948. Among its many stars were Hank Williams, Johnny Cash, Elvis Presley, and Jim Reeves

Louvin Brothers Ira (1924-65) and Charlie (1927-) were famed in the 1950s and early 1960s for their superb close harmony duets of mainly gospel songs. They split up in 1964, and within a few months Ira was killed in a head-on auto crash 80

Lynn, Loretta (1935-) Born Loretta Webb, the coalminer's daughter was one of eight children who grew up in poverty. By the later 1960s she had won a closetful of awards, including three times Female Vocalist of the Year. Her autobiography was also a bestseller 109, 111, *129*, 150

McAuliffe, Leon (1917-) Member of the Light Crust Doughboys who later joined Bob Wills with the Texas Playboys. Composer of ***Steel Guitar Rag,*** he was one of the first to use that instrument in country music 64

McCoy, Charlie (1941-) Multi-instrumentalist who specializes on harmonica. A solo artist who is much in demand as a session man *130*

McCurry, Clarence Earl. *See* ASHLEY, Clarence 'Tom'

McGee, Sam and Kirk Sam (1894-1975) and Kirk (1899-) first appeared with Uncle Dave Macon and the Fruit Jar Drinkers in 1926. In the 1930s they joined Fiddlin' Arthur Smith and later joined Bill Monroe's band. They became a separate act in the 1950s 31, 32

McMichen, Clayton 'Pappy' (1900-70) Superb oldtime fiddler whose pop-orientated, jazz-influenced licks helped to make the Skillet Lickers the most outstanding string band of the late 1920s and 1930s. He was also a songwriter and comedian, and later formed his own bands 8, 10

McReynolds, Jim and Jesse. *See* JIM AND JESSE

McWilliams, Elsie Sister of Jimmie Rodgers who co-wrote with him many of his best songs. *See* RODGERS, Jimmie

Macon, Dorris Son of Uncle Dave Macon. *See* MACON, Uncle Dave

Macon, Uncle Dave (David Harrison) [1870-1952] Known as the Dixie Dewdrop, he was the first great star of the Grand Ole Opry. A talented banjoist, comedian, and all-round entertainer, usually helped by his son Dorris on stage, he was appreciated and loved throughout the nation 29-32, *41*

Mainer, J E (1898-1971) Oldtime fiddler and leader of a famous string band of the 1930s, the Mountaineers. They recorded more than 200 sides and broadcast over 140 radio stations. His younger brother, Wade, was part of the band until 1936, when the new group was renamed the Crazy Mountaineers 10, 13, *16*

Mainer, Wade (1907-) Younger brother of JE, who split from his brother in 1936 to form the Sons of the Mountaineers. He had a distinctive mountain voice and an innovative two-finger banjo technique *9,* 13

Mandrell, Barbara (1948-) One of the top contemporary country and pop female artists, she is a multi-instrumentalist with a fine voice and very easy on the eye. Won the CMA Entertainer of the Year award two years in succession *166-7*

Man in Black. *See* CASH, Johnny

Kris Kristofferson

Uncle Dave Macon

Martin, Jimmy (James Henry) [1927-] Bluegrass guitarist and lead vocalist who originally appeared with Bill Monroe's band. He left to form his own group, the Sunny Mountain Boys which, although riddled with prestigious performers, was not above using drums, to the horror of the purists *75, 77*

Martin, Lecil Travis. *See* BOXCAR WILLIE

Marvin, Ken *See* LONZO AND OSCAR

Maynard, Ken (1895-1973) Fiddler, banjoist, singer, rodeo star, and movie actor, he was the first cowboy to sing on film. Gene Autry made his debut in 1934 in **In Old Santa Fe,** one of Maynard's films *50, 58*

Miller, Roger (1936-) Popular writer and performer of catchy and sometimes zany country and pop songs. Has written smash hits for Ray Price, George Jones, and others. Won a unique tally of six Grammies in 1965 *132-3*

Milsap, Ronnie (1946-) Blind from birth, he became one of the most popular country and pop entertainers of the 1970s and 1980s. Talented pianist, violinist, cellist, and guitarist, he has won a closetful of awards since the late 1970s *156, 156*

Monroe, Bill (William Smith) [1911-] The Father of Bluegrass started off with his elder brother Charlie in 1934 on radio as the Monroe Brothers. They split in 1938 and Bill formed his own band, the Blue Grass Boys. His masterly mandolin playing and high tenor voice eventually established a definitive style which he called 'bluegrass' *39, 41, 66, 68, 69*

Monroe, Charlie (1903-) Elder brother of Bill and who with him formed the Monroe Brothers, a pioneer bluegrass duo. Charlie went his own way in 1938 to form the Kentucky Pardners, without the success of his younger brother *39, 41, 69*

Montgomery, Melba (1938-) Strong-voiced Tennessee singer who spent her first four professional years touring with Roy Acuff. After a successful solo debut in 1962 she also had hits with a succession of duetists, including George Jones, Charlie Louvin, and Gene Pitney *157, 158-9*

Mullican, Aubrey 'Moon' (1909-67) Bluesy pianist with an innovative two-finger piano style. Known as the King of the Hillbilly Piano Players, his career extended from the late 1930s to the 1960s with revamped hits such as **Jole Blon** and **Goodnight Irene** *64*

Murray, Anne (1946-) Popular Canadian crossover artist who was raised with a classical musical education. Her light, appealing voice took **Snowbird** right into the charts in 1970 *142, 158, 162*

Nashville sound Style of country music created in the Nashville studios in the 1960s that tended to move away from the hardline traditionalist sound of fiddle, guitar, and banjo and more towards the pop sound of lush strings, steel guitars, and percussion. Purely commercial in intent, it was headed by Chet Atkins and eventually made Nashville the country music capital of the world *112*

Nelson, Rick (1940-) Country rocker whose chequered career has included two popular albums issued in the 1960s, **Country Fever** and **Bright Lights and Country Music** *169*

Nelson, Willie (1933-) Legendary singer/songwriter who struggled for years to gain acceptance of his anarchic ways. Eventually won recognition as a leader of the 'outlaws'. Initiated the annual Dripping Springs festivals, a mix of traditional and contemporary acts *138, 138, 139, 139*

Newman, Jimmy 'C' (1927-) Prominent Cajun singer and fiddler who tinges a traditional Cajun style with contemporary country. **Cry, Cry Darling** (1954) was his first hit *82, 83, 83*

Nitty Gritty Dirt Band California-based country rock band who in 1971 made recording history with traditionalist elders such as Roy Acuff, Mother Maybelle Carter, Doc Watson, Merle Travis, Earl Scruggs, Jimmy Martin, and others to cut a triple album called **Will the Circle Be Unbroken.** The unlikely amalgam was a classic success *46*

Nolan, Bob (1908-80) Leader of the Sons of the Pioneers who flourished from the 1930s to the 1950s. Credited with the invention of western harmony singing, he composed such enormous hits as **Cool Water** and **Tumbling Tumbleweeds** *56*

Norris, Fate Oldtime banjoist and original member of the Skillet Lickers. *See* SKILLET LICKERS

North Carolina Ramblers Oldtime string band led by Charlie Poole. *See* POOLE, CHARLIE

Bill Monroe

Oak Ridge Boys A popular gospel group until the mid-1970s, they evolved from The Country Cut-Ups, who performed at Oak Ridge atomic energy plant during World War II. After they changed to country, they also gained millions of pop fans with *Elvira* in 1981 158

Opryland Musical theme park a few miles outside Nashville that now houses the Grand Ole Opry in its Opry Theater. Opryland opened in 1972 and covers 120 acres   26, *27,* 34, 35

Osborne Brothers Bob (1931-) and Sonny (1937-) formed a duo in the 1950s, and later added a third member (the first of these being Benny Birchfield) to sing and play progressive bluegrass that became popular in the 1960s. Bob sang tenor and played mandolin; Sonny sang baritone and played banjo   *74,* 75

Oswald, Bashful Brother Born Beecher 'Pete' Kirby, has been a guitarist, banjoist, and dobro player of distinction for many years. One of Acuff's famed Smokey Mountain Boys, he appeared in bib-overall, played dobro with the band, but preferred banjo for solo work   44, *99*

Outlaws, The A faction of country music's singer/songwriters who in the early 1960s flaunted the conventional, established Nashville pattern to go their own way in writing and performance. Unfamiliar attitudes, tones, and phrases helped to give new dimensions to many old favorites. Leaders of the new movement were Willie Nelson and Waylon Jennings 138

Owens, Buck (Alvis Edgar) [1929-   ] Guitarist and singer/songwriter, he was one of the trendsetters to come out of California in the 1960s. At one time he had 19 No 1s out of 39 titles in the charts. Helped to make Bakersfield an alternative country music center to Nashville   *121,* 128-9, 134

Ozark Jubilee Show. *See* FOLEY, Red

Parsons, Gram (1946-73) Country-rock pioneer who died aged 26 at the peak of his powers from a heart attack induced by drink and drugs. While a member of The Byrds and later the Flying Burritos, influenced both groups with his country leanings   146

Parton, Dolly Rebecca (1946-   ) Talented singer/songwriter whose appealing voice and eyecatching figure have shot her to the peak of international stardom. Much of her success stems from her earlier association with the Porter Wagoner Show   132, 142, *144,* 145

Pearl, Minnie (Sarah Colley) [1912-   ] An Opry regular for nearly 50 years, the Queen of Country Comedy has become instantly recognizable with her 'Howdeee!' greeting, country dress and floral hat   *94,* 97

Peer, Ralph Sylvester (1892-1960) Outstanding talent scout of the 1920s for Okeh, and later Victor. Among his many triumphs were the recording of Fiddlin' John Carson, Jimmie Rodgers, and the Carter Family   8-10, *14,* 16, 18, 20, 23

Pennick, Mary Frances. *See* DAVIS, Skeeter

Perkins, Luther Longtime guitarist with Johnny Cash. Burned to death in 1969. *See* CASH, Johnny

Pierce, Webb (1926-   ) Guitarist and singer who came out of the Louisiana Hayride in the 1950s to popularize the sound of the steel guitar. Joined the Opry with Red Sovine   *118,* 119

Poindexter, Albert. *See* DEXTER, Al

Poole, Charlie (1892-1931) Pioneer banjo player and singer, and leader of the North Carolina Ramblers, one of the most popular string bands of the 1920s   13-15

Possum Hunters String band of the 1920s. *See* BATE, Dr Humphry

Pozo Seco Singers. *See* WILLIAMS, Don

Presley, Elvis (1935-77) King of rock 'n' roll, whose recordings began with blues and rockabilly. In the 1950s appeared on the Louisiana Hayride and the Grand Ole Opry. Also toured with Hank Snow and Johnny Cash   66, *107, 108,* 112, 130, 142

Preston, Terry. *See* HUSKY, Ferlin

Price, Ray (1926-   ) Contemporary pop singer who did much to establish the Nashville sound in the 1960s. Originally a hillbilly singer in the Hank Williams mold, his chart successes ran into many million-sellers   138

Pride, Charley (1938-   ) Ex-cottonpicker who by the 1970s had become an international superstar and easily the most successful and wealthiest black country artist of all time. His warm, low-key baritone voice has helped him make more than 40 albums and 50 singles   32, 91, 148, *170, 171*

Puckett, (George) Riley (1894-1946) Oldtime blind singer and guitarist and featured singer in the 1920s and 1930s in Gid Tanner's Skillet Lickers. First man to yodel on record   10, *11,* 13

Pugh, Wynette. *See* WYNETTE, Tammy

Jimmy Martin

Willie Nelson

Dolly Parton

Ray, Billy Banjo player with the Kentucky Colonels. *See* KENTUCKY COLONELS

Rector, Red First generation bluegrass mandolin player. Played and recorded with Bill Clifton. *See* CLIFTON, Bill

Reed, Jerry (1937-) Born Jerry Hubbard, this ex-session guitarist, songwriter, and movie actor graduated from rockabilly to become one of Nashville's finest pickers. His songs have been recorded by artists such as Presley and Gene Vincent   *126,* 129-30

Reeves, Jim (James Travis) [1923-64] Pop ballad singer Gentleman Jim Reeves was originally a DJ, but his easy-listening voice was found to blend perfectly with the emerging Nashville sound of the early 1960s. Since his death in a plane crash, has become something of a cult figure   91, *91-2*

Reno and Smiley Bluegrass duo of the 1950s and 1960s, backed by the Tennessee Cut-ups. Banjoist Reno later joined Arthur 'Guitar Boogie' Smith   77, 78, *78*

Rich, Charlie (1934-) The Silver Fox started out as a jazz and blues singer. In 1973 the release of his album ***Behind Closed Doors*** brought him superstardom and launched an urbane, middle-of-the-road sound that has since been dubbed 'countrypolitan'   150, *151,* 152

Riley, Jeannie C (1945-) Born Jeannie Stephenson, she sang in talent shows without success and worked as a secretary. One record, the Tom T Hall song, ***Harper Valley PTA,*** in 1968, changed all that and shot her to stardom with millions of copies sold   148

Rinzler, Ralph Prestigious musicologist and one-time mandolin player and singer with bluegrass group the Greenbriar Boys   77

Ritter, Tex (Woodward Maurice) [1905-74] Highly popular singing cowboy and Hollywood actor whose authentic projection of Western life made up for an indifferent voice. Won an Academy Award for his rendering of the theme song of ***High Noon*** in 1953   *55,* 56, 58, *90,* 112

Robbins, Marty (1925-84) Learnt cowboy and old Western songs from his grandfather, a traveling medicine man. His long career of hits started in 1953 and included million-sellers ***Devil Woman*** and ***El Paso***   *96,* 97

Robertson, Alexander 'Eck' Campbell (1887-) Oldtime Texas fiddler and a strong claimant for being one of the first country musicians to be recorded. He and his friend, Henry

C Gilliland, cut six titles for Victor in 1922   8

Robison, Carson J (1890-1957) Ingenious and witty songwriter and performer, he began broadcasting and recording in the early 1920s and carried on until his death in 1957. Author of *Barnacle Bill the Sailor, Life Gets Teejus* and other hits, he also partnered Vernon Dalhart and Frank Luther, besides forming many bands of his own   8, *23*

Rodgers, Carrie Widow of Jimmie Rodgers. *See* TUBB, Ernest

Rodgers, Jimmie (James Charles) [1897-1933] Variously known as the Father of Country Music and the Singing Brakeman, he wrote and performed a succession of blues, folk, earthy, and country music in the 1920s and early 1930s. Revered by country fans worldwide, he became the first member of the Country Music Hall of Fame   16-18, *16, 19,* 20, 21, 23, *24,* 25, 35

Rodriguez, Johnny (Juan Raul) [1952-] Chicano singer/songwriter guitarist, was discovered by Bobby Bare and Tom T Hall. His first hit was *Pass Me By* (1972)   *159,* 162, 165

Rogers, Kenny (1938-) Millionaire pop-orientated country singer who went from the New Christy Minstrels to the First Edition. For a time sang successful duets with Dottie West. But his solo effort, *Lucille,* in 1977, made him a superstar   145-6, *168*

Rogers, Roy (1911-) Born Leonard Slye, the King of the Cowboys made more than 100 Western movies. Formed the Sons of the Pioneers with Bob Nolan and Tim Spencer. Later with his wife, Dale Evans, concentrated on gospel music and other religious material   53, 54-56, *60, 61, 62, 63*

Rogers, Will (William Penn Adair) [1897-1935] World famous philosopher, author, and humorist, who encouraged Jimmie Rodgers and Gene Autrey at the start of their careers   *24,* 52

Ronstadt, Linda (1946-) Country rock star who in 1975 was voted third most popular female star of the nation. With her roots in folk music, she combined with the musicians who later became known as The Eagles, on her third album, *Linda Ronstadt*   159, 160, *160*

Rorer, Posey Crippled ex-coalminer fiddler who, with Charlie Poole and Norman Woodlieff, recorded as the North Carolina Ramblers in 1925   15

Rose, Fred (1897-1954) Co-founder with Roy Acuff of the Acuff-Rose publishing empire, he was a professional pianist and wrote many famous songs. Among the stars he discovered was Hank Williams   44

Rutherford, Leonard Oldtime fiddler from Kentucky who in 1914 formed a partnership with blind banjo-playing singer/songwriter Dick Burnett. They recorded their first songs in 1926   15

Scruggs, Earl (Eugene) [1924-] One half of the famous bluegrass partnership of Flatt and Scruggs, he revolutionized the three-finger method of banjo playing. As a result, bluegrass reached a new peak in popularity and Earl became the world's most famous banjoist. When the partnership dissolved in 1969 Scruggs went on to form a progressive bluegrass group, the Earl Scruggs Revue   16, 66, *68,* 69, *71,* 80, 81

Shepard, Jean (1933-) Popular female vocalist since the 1950s, she is devoted to keeping country music free from the influence of pop. One of her great hits was the duet with Ferlin Husky, *Dear John Letter* (1953)   121

Sheppard, Audrey Mae First wife of Hank Williams. *See* WILLIAMS, Hank

Sherrill, Billy Vice-President of CBS in Nashville and one-time producer of the smooth, middle-of-the-road country sound in the 1960s that came to be known as 'countrypolitan'   124

Silver Fox. *See* RICH, Charlie

Skaggs, Ricky (1954-) Multi-instrumentalist and juvenile prodigy who was raised on gospel, traditional, and bluegrass music. As a child, he appeared with Flatt and Scruggs and later with the Stanley Brothers. He became a star member of Emmylou Harris' Hot Band, and when he left, formed his own group. They now play a mixture of bluegrass with electric contemporary overtones   134, *172-3*

Skillet Lickers An important and extremely influential string band of the 1920s and 1930s. It was led by Gid Tanner with the support of Clayton McMichen and Riley Puckett   10

Slaughter, Marion Try. *See* DALHART, Vernon

Smith, Fiddlin' Arthur (1898-) Pioneer fiddler from Tennessee who in the early 1930s joined Sam and Kirk McGee to form the Dixieliners. He later recorded with the Delmore Brothers and formed his own Arthur Smith Trio   32

Smokey Mountain Boys Band formed by Roy Acuff. *See* ACUFF, Roy

Snow, Clarence Eugene 'Hank' (1914-) Canadian singer/songwriter and guitarist who scored more than 60 hits between 1950 and 1970. His self-penned *I'm Moving On* (1950) stayed in the country charts for more than 40 weeks   21, 112, *113,* 114, *114*

Sons of the Pioneers Early cowboy string band that evolved from the Pioneer Trio, made up of Roy Rogers, Bob Nolan and Tim Spencer in 1934. They made many records, broadcast frequently, and appeared in several Roy Rogers films   56

Elvis Presley

✫ ✫

Kenny Rogers

Sovine, Red (Woodrow Wilson) [1918-] Country entertainer and singer of trucking and CB radio songs. Was a leading light of the Louisiana Hayride when he replaced Hank Williams there. Joined the Opry in 1954 and recorded successful duets with Webb Pierce 148

Spears, Billie Jo (1937-) Crossover artist with the voice of a bluesy nightclub singer, she recorded her first number, *Too Old for Toys, Too Young for Boys,* at age 13. Her big break came in 1975 with *Blanket on the Ground,* since which she has scored a number of other chart entries 148-50, *150*

Sprague, Carl T (1895-) The original Singing Cowboy, was inspired by Vernon Dalhart's *The Prisoner's Song* to record 10 songs for Victor in 1925. Among them was *When the Work's All Done This Fall,* which sold almost a million copies 48

Stanley Brothers Carter Glen (1926-66) and Ralph Edmond (1927-), two of the finest bluegrass musicians ever recorded. Carter was the guitarist and lead vocalist, Ralph the banjoist and harmony vocalist. They began as an oldtime harmony duo, but switched to a bluegrass style in 1948. After Carter's death in 1966, Ralph carried on alone with their backing group the Clinch Mountain Boys 70, *70,* 72, 80

Statesiders, The. *See* TILLIS, Mel

Statler Brothers Lew De Witt (1938-), Philip Balsley (1939-), Harold Reid (1939-), and Don Reid (1945-), only two of them are brothers, became one of the most successful vocal groups in country music history. Initially a gospel group inspired by the Blackwood Brothers, they turned to country and became part of the Johnny Cash Show 158, *165*

Stevens, Ray A pop country artist whose clever humorous ditties include *Bridget the Midget* and *The Streak* 157, *157*

★ ★

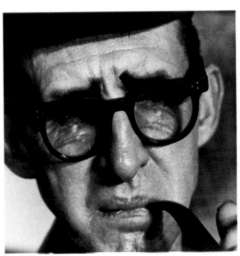

Stringbean

Slim Whitman

Tucker, Tanya Denise (1958-)
Teenage prodigy whose singing talents
were first heard as a 13-year-old on
Delta Dawn. Provocative pop records
such as *Would You Lay with Me* (1975)
followed, but her later efforts were
more rock-influenced 154, *154, 155,*
156
Twitty, Conway (1933-) Born
Harold Lloyd Jenkins, he took his
professional name from two obscure
townships. Originally a rock 'n' roll
artist, he turned towards country in the
1960s and proceeded to collect an
enormous number of hits, including
some famous duets with Loretta Lynn
150, *151*

W

Wagoner, Porter (1930-) Popular
entertainer and showman who began
his own syndicated TV series in 1961.
Originally it featured Norma Jean but
she was later replaced by Dolly Parton,
who made some notable duets with
Porter *129,* 130-2, 145
Wakely, Jimmy (James Clarence)
[1914-] Durable vocalist and movie
actor who first came to public notice on
Gene Autry's Melody Ranch show in
the 1940s. Later formed his own band,
which included Cliffie Stone, Merle
Travis, and Spade Cooley. Appeared in
more than 50 movies and scored a
tremendous hit dueting with Margaret
Whiting in Tillman's *Slippin' Around*
58, 59, 112
Waller, Charlie. *See* COUNTRY
GENTLEMEN
Watson, Arthel 'Doc' (1923-)
Legendary blind folk and country
guitarist, banjoist and singer, was
raised on the music of the Carter
Family and Gid Tanner. His down-to-
earth, homely approach and musical
virtuosity on guitar have earned him a

large and devoted following 112
Webb, Brenda Gayle. *See* GAYLE,
Crystal
Wells, Kitty (1919-) Born Muriel
Deason, the Queen of Country Music
has made a deep and lasting impact on
country music. Before joining the Opry
in 1952, she was one of the great stars
of the Louisiana Hayride. In 16 years
she recorded 57 hit singles, and was
voted top female singer for 12 years in
succession 92, *92, 93,* 94
West, Dottie (Dorothy Marie)
[1932-] A member of the Opry since
1964, she majored in classical music.
Working in nightclubs at first, she
scored her first hit for RCA in 1963, *Let*
Me Off at the Corner. Her big success
was *Here Comes My Baby,* made
famous by Perry Como. She has
written more than 400 songs, some of
them commercial jingles
Whispering Bill. *See* ANDERSON, Bill
White, Clarence Legendary guitarist
of the Kentucky Colonels. *See* KENTUCKY
COLONELS
White, Mary Widow of Jim Reeves.
See REEVES, Jim
White, Roland Brother of Clarence and
mandolin player with the Kentucky
Colonels. *See* KENTUCKY COLONELS
Whitman, Slim (1924-) Born Otis
Dewey Whitman Jnr, yodeling,

falsetto-voiced balladeer whose
popularity seems to have been greater
in England than in his own country. His
renditions of *Indian Love Call, Rose*
Marie, and similar romantic offerings
have gained him many awards 114,
115, 117
Whitter, William Henry (1892-1941)
Pioneer recording artist who sang, and
played organ, piano, guitar, harmonica,
and fiddle. Was first recorded in 1923,
but his first releases came almost a
year later. Formed his own band,
Whitter's Virginia Breakdowners, and in
1927 teamed up successfully with blind
fiddler George Banman Grayson 9
Williams, Don (1939-) Voted 1980
Country Artist of the Decade by British
fans, he began his professional career
by forming the Pozo Seco Singers in
1964, with a mixture of country, pop,
and folk. Later, his solo hits such as
You're My Best Friend and *I Recall a*
Gypsy Woman, were delivered with a
winning cool, laid-back style 146,
147-8, *148, 149*
Williams, Hank (Hiram King) [1923-53]
Composer and singer whose
popularity and influence on country
music was perhaps equaled only by
that of Jimmie Rodgers. A moody,
illiterate alcoholic, he nevertheless
managed to compose songs of such

Hank Williams

Tammy Wynette

PICTURE CREDITS

Click Chicago Joe Viesti 18, 18-19, 25, 81 right, 82-83 **Columbia Records** 169 right **Country Music Foundation** title page far left, 6-12, 14, 16, 19 bottom, 20 bottom, 22 right, 23, 28-29, 30, 33, 38, 39 bottom, 41 middle, 42, 45, 46 bottom, 50 bottom, 51 bottom, 53 top, 61 top, 62, 68 top, 69, 70 top, 71, 73 left, 74, 75, 86, 88-90, 93, 95, 98, 102, 103, 108 bottom, 118 bottom, 120, 131 bottom, 179-181, 182 right, 184, 189 **Billy Deaton Talent Agency** 115, 190 top **Ronald Grant Collection** 53 bottom, 54, 55, 58, 59, 60, 61 bottom **The Image Bank** H J Anders 19 top, Ira Block 13 top, Garry Gay title page, Ellis Herwig 81, John Lee contents page, 139, Peter Miller 20 top, F Roiter 13 bottom, Peter Runyon 48, F Sirven half title, Harald Sund 17 left, **London Features International** title page far right, 78, 92, 113, 129 bottom, 133 bottom, 135, 138, 145, 150, 157 right, 159 top, 160, 162, 164 top, 171 **MCA Records** 68 bottom, 147 bottom, 183 **Pictorial Press** 91 **Sylvia Pitcher** 21 right, 26, 31, 36-37, 87 **RCA Records** 137 top **David Redfern** 47, 72, 79, 80, 83, 96, 105, 116, 118 top, 123, 124, 127, 128, 129 top, 130, 131 top, 132, 133 top, 142 left, 143, 144, 147 top, 148, 149, 151 bottom, 156, 158 top, 159 bottom, 163, 164 bottom, 170, 172-173, 177 top, 178 bottom, 186 **Rex Features Limited** 22 left, 49, 107 **Tony Stone Associates** 39 top, 43, 50 top, 51 top, 63-67, 82 **Transworld Feature Syndicate** title page left, 76-77, 137 bottom, 142 right, 154, 155, 166-168, 182 left, 188

All other pictures courtesy **Bob Powel/Country Music People**

Front Cover: London Features International bottom left and right David Redfern main picture Frank Spooner Pictures top left

Back Cover: London Features International

Multimedia Publications (UK) Limited have endeavored to observe the legal requirements with regard to the supplier of photographic material.

Endpapers:
A glittering array of showbiz talent greets packed audiences in Nashville's famed Opryland.